WANT MY HELP IM[...]
THE CONTENT OF [...] BOOK?

My mission is to help you connect with your high-level spirit guides and receive their guidance.

That's why I wrote this book.

If you'd like my assistance in implementing the content of this book, then book a FREE Discovery Call with me here:

talktoyourspiritguides.com/call

The purpose of this call is to find out how I can best support you and if we're a good match for each other.

There are no obligations to this call. Hence, if you feel that there is no fit after doing this call, there will be no pressure to take up any of my services.

I will always keep your information 100% private and confidential.

YOUR FREE BONUS

I have a free bonus to thank you for purchasing this book. It's a one-page cheat sheet of my "Ten-Step Method to Spirit Communication" for you to print out and support your practice.

I'd like to share this cheat sheet with you. To access it, sign up for my email list on my free bonus page (see the link below), and you'll immediately receive it in your inbox.

You'll also receive my weekly newsletter, "The Humble Observer," every Saturday. It includes tips to raise your vibration and connect with your spirit guides, exclusive free content like guided meditations, plus special offers, first dibs on live events, and other fabulous perks. *I guarantee 100% privacy. Your information will not be shared.*

Please sign up using this URL, it only takes a second:

talktoyourspiritguides.com/bonus

Once you have signed up, you'll immediately receive access to the cheat sheet.

I'm happy to have you on my list and excited for us to start our spirit communication journey together!

With love,
Will

"How To Talk To Your Spirit Guides" by Will Almando

ISBN: 978-2-0648-1582-0

Cover page and book design by Nicolas Beron.

TalkToYourSpiritGuides.com

TO YOU

May this book inspire you to frequently talk to your family of spirit guides and apply their advice. They offer unconditional love, protection, and guidance to help you implement positive changes in your life, fulfill your soul's plan, and walk toward Self-Realization.

TO MY PARENTS

You have always wanted and supported my two sisters and me to follow our dreams, explore our interests, strive for excellence, engage in meaningful relationships, and continue the legacy of our ancestors. I'm grateful for your love and everything you taught me during and after your earthly incarnations.

TO MY CHILDREN

You have been the light of my life since the day you were born. Thank you for all your teachings and inspiration. I will always be there for you and support you. I love you to the moon and back!

TO MARISOL

Thank you so much for coming into my life as my cherished perfect mirror and walking with me toward the rising sun. I love you forever!

TO SUZANNA "GURUMAA"

I humbly bow to the Divine in You in deep gratitude and obeisance!

TO MY SPIRIT GUIDE FAMILY

Thank you from the bottom of my heart for your unconditional love, blessings, guidance, support, and protection!

Table of Contents

1.
Introduction

Talking to my spirit guides has changed my life in many positive ways. I hope it will change yours, too!

I was an anxious, depressed, fearful, and angry workaholic with several addictions. I was totally frustrated with my life. I felt like I had built my own prison from which I couldn't escape.

Thanks to my connection with my spirit guides, I started to follow their recommendations to tear down the walls of my imaginary prison. That allowed me to gradually get rid of all the anxiety, depression, fear, anger, and addictions in the last few years.

These personal and spiritual developments only became possible after I intensified my spirit communication and decided to really implement their advice.

Today, under their constant guidance, I'm building my dream life and following my sacred spiritual path.

I have written this book to introduce you to my "Ten-Step Method," which anyone can use to connect and talk to their spirit guides.

This book also provides all the information you need to stay grounded, safe, and protected, increase your frequency, and go deeper toward constant connection. It aims to answer all your lingering questions about spirit communication.

Whether you have already listened and talked to them or not, **several high-level spirit guides constantly work on your**

behalf. They have always loved, encouraged, and supported you since your birth.

Spirit communication is a skill that anyone can learn. You don't need to go through intermediates like psychic mediums or gurus to receive guidance from your spirit guides.

You don't need to be born with "special gifts," as some mediums claim. Everyone can learn to talk to their spirit guides, just like everyone can learn to play the piano.

There are no prerequisites or requirements. You don't need years of meditation experience. Mastering spirit communication only requires time, dedication to practice, and the right approach, which you will learn in this book.

You can immediately apply the ten simple steps to start talking to your high-level spirit guides and angels today! Using my "Ten-Step Method," you will always remain **safe, conscious, and in complete control**. You don't need to enter a trance to communicate with your spirit guides.

They'll always respect your free will. They'll never force anything upon you. They'll show you different aspects of your situation and scenarios and the likely consequences of your decisions. They'll give you ideas, inspiration for your projects, and wise advice to overcome challenges.

They'll encourage you to step out of your comfort zone, share your gifts with the world, and find your purpose in this lifetime. They want you to be blissfully happy. They will lead you toward experiencing good health, joy, freedom, abundance, and love.

Learning to talk to our spirit guides accelerates our spiritual growth. Regular spirit communication allows our lives to fall into patterns of ease and flow, reducing our resistance and making our time on Earth endlessly delightful.

Your spirit guides want you to experience everything your soul decided for before your birth, to implement your "soul plan."

Their ultimate wish is that you find out who you really are on your path to full Self-Realization.

My Journey with My Spirit Guides

I have developed and applied the "Ten-Step Method" for my spirit communication for more than 25 years. I learned the first parts of it in the 1990s in a seminar as a form of channeling, allowing spirit entities to speak through me.

I was surprised by how easy channeling was and how well it worked for the other participants and me. After that seminar, I continued to channel spirit entities once in a while and recorded some of those sessions.

A couple of years later, I went on an extended trip to Asia. The first stop was a 10-day silent Vipassana retreat in a Buddhist monastery in southern Thailand, which was a totally incredible and life-changing experience for me.

Everything slowed down for me during that retreat. We spent almost all of our time in silent meditation and contemplation. After the first three days, I entered a deeply peaceful state.

I felt how open my channels were and quietly started applying the channeling method I had previously learned during many of the meditation sessions. I had to maintain silence, so I could not let the spirit entities speak through me this time.

Due to my profound meditative state, connecting with spirit entities felt easier. I met my first high-level spirit guide called "Niaku." He had a very intense and powerful presence. It felt wonderful to let him enter into my energy field and feel his sublime strength.

I asked him many questions, and he patiently replied to all of them. He also took me on several visual journeys.

In one of those, he showed me the immense suffering of various people all over the world. Many of them were complaining and crying about the hardships of their human existence.

He explained how following the sacred spiritual path is the only way out of human suffering, gradually letting go of our desires and wants as well as our fears and "don't wants."

This approach was utterly congruent with the "middle way" Buddhist teaching I received at the retreat.

After spending more time in Thailand, I took a six-month backpacking trip through India. I didn't plan this journey. I talked to Niaku daily, and he always directed me where to go.

Under his guidance and protection, I traveled from the estuary of the holy river Ganges near Calcutta to its source in Gangotri in the Himalayas, with a big detour via the southernmost tip of India in Tamil Nadu and other southern states.

Along the way, I enjoyed many amazing encounters and spiritual experiences. I'm still extremely grateful to Niaku for his precious guidance on this journey and far beyond.

Life happened after I returned to my home country of Switzerland and later lived in South Africa. I continued to practice spirit communication occasionally and met other extraordinary high-level guides.

But sometimes, I forgot to talk to my spirit guide family for extended periods, burying myself in work and other duties.

Whenever a crisis occurred or I faced a challenge, I asked for their guidance again. They have always given me invaluable advice.

I became a disciple of an ancient Kundalini lineage in 2020 and committed to daily Yoga, meditation, and spirit communication practices. In spite of that, I went through a very depressive period during the Covid pandemic.

I strongly intensified my spirit communication since I first traveled to Mexico in early 2022. I focused on my meditation practice and encountered a spirit guide called "Sanskinani."

Sanskinani took me on fabulous journeys to the deepest depths and highest heights. She led me to open my heart, forgive myself and others, and connect from heart to heart with the people I met and with animal messengers.

Sanskinani kickstarted my healing process from my anxiety, depression, and addictions. Under her guidance, I immensely enjoyed the magic of the Oaxacan coast and the Pacific Ocean.

With Sanskinani, my spirit communication became a constant connection for the first time. Even when not in one of my daily active sessions, I started receiving her immediate answers to my questions.

She asked me to share my method of spirit communication with the world. I immediately introduced it to several friends I had met.

This experience helped me extend and fine-tune the "Ten-Step Method" into its present form presented in this book.

Soon after returning from this trip, I decided to emigrate to Mexico. I now live in magical Yucatan, where I met a powerful spirit guide called "El Cateño."

He led me to meet a wonderful traditional Mayan shaman and discover the ancient spiritual practices of the Mayans. He has supported me all the way in continuing my healing journey and writing this book.

I'm very grateful for the love, wisdom, guidance, and protection I receive daily from my spirit guides. I want you to receive the same and overcome all your challenges with your spiritual guidance.

An Overview of What You'll Learn

You'll learn everything you need to know about spirit communication:

- Who and what high-level spirit guides are
- What you can ask your spirit guides
- How they talk to you
- How you can ensure safety in spirit communication
- When and where to practice
- How to ground yourself
- How to raise your frequency
- How to connect with your guides and talk to them in ten steps
- How to overcome blockages
- How to go deeper toward constant connection and a guided life

This book is only about personal, private communication with high-level spirit guides. It does not cover giving psychic or spiritual readings to others, which I'd recommend only after specific training.

May learning my "Ten-Step Method" to talk to your spirit guides help you implement positive changes in your life, follow your soul's sacred plan, and find love, peace, and happiness!

2.
Why Should You Talk
To Your Spirit Guides?

Consciously connecting with your family of high-level spirit guides is one of the most precious gifts you can give yourself.

They offer you a **timeless relationship of unconditional love and friendship**. Unlike most human relationships, there are no strings attached.

There are no conditions, no obligations, no expectations. They'll never be disappointed by you or angry at you.

They have supported you since birth and are always there for you to talk to them. They have been waiting for you to open up to them, allowing them to help you even better.

They are more than happy to help you with everything that matters to you. They want you to find your true purpose in this lifetime and walk along your sacred path toward Self-Realization.

They want you to discover the glowing light within yourself. They wish for you to shine brightly and share your light with others.

The world needs such leaders in its present turmoil. With the support of your spirit guides, you can be one of them.

They offer you a shield of protection from physical, emotional, and spiritual harm. They wish you to tune in and listen to them so you can make the right choices to protect yourself, providing a sense of safety and reassurance.

They offer wise advice on your personal development and spiritual path, as well as practical, mundane matters. You can ask them any questions, and they'll reply immediately to the best of their abilities, providing constant guidance and support.

Connecting with your spirit guides is a powerful tool for personal growth and development. They support you in overcoming obstacles, healing past traumas, and navigating life transitions. They can also help you tap into your intuition, discover your life's purpose, and align your actions with your spiritual beliefs.

Through their guidance, you'll embark on a journey of self-discovery and improvement. They help you to let go of fear, worry, and doubt, empowering you and boosting your confidence. You'll receive insights and solutions to your challenges and never feel alone again!

Talking to your spirit guides enhances your spiritual growth and awareness.

Spirit communication practice helps strengthen your connection to the Divine and supports you in discovering who you are. Regular practice also increases your intuition and psychic abilities in other areas.

Connecting with your spirit guides can significantly improve your relationships, too. You'll develop increased empathy, understanding, and patience. They may lead you to meet valuable new friends and even soulmates.

By releasing energetic baggage and healing emotional wounds under their guidance, your connections with others will become healthier.

They support you in choosing relationships that align with your spiritual growth. Some people may exit your life during this process, creating space for new meaningful contacts.

Talking to your spirit guides also enriches your connection with nature. You'll develop a heightened awareness of the beauty and sacredness of the natural world and the interconnectedness of all living beings.

They promote environmental stewardship, instilling a sense of responsibility and a commitment to sustainable living. They emphasize the importance of spending time outdoors, letting you observe and connect with nature.

Spirit guides encourage embracing and expressing gratitude, allowing you to shift your focus from what may be lacking to acknowledging the abundance already present in your life.

Gratitude is a powerful energy that attracts positivity, allowing you to recognize the beauty in everyday moments. Focusing on gratitude for the positive aspects of a situation will develop stronger resilience, making it easier to navigate your life's ups and downs.

I invite you to discover the wonderful, loving relationships your spirit guides offer you. Walk on your unique, sacred path toward reaching your ultimate potential and fulfilling your purpose in this lifetime.

What Your Spirit Guides Will NOT Do For You

Your high-level spirit guides do a lot to support you, but there are a few things that they can't do:

Interference with free will

They always respect the principle of free will. They will never interfere with your ability to make free choices or decisions. The responsibility for your actions ultimately rests with you.

Predicting future events

While your spirit guides can provide insights into potential paths and outcomes, they don't predict future events precisely.

The future is dynamic and influenced by numerous variables, including free will choices and external factors.

Physical healing

They are non-physical entities that cannot directly intervene in the physical world. They offer guidance for your health and well-being and may assist you in activating your healing powers.

However, you and your health providers remain responsible for your physical health.

Material gain or wealth accumulation

Your spirit guides may offer insights into prosperity and tapping into abundance, but they do not focus on material gain.

Direct requests for financial success or material wealth are beyond their scope. They won't gift you a brand-new Cadillac.

Forcing a change in others

High-level Spirit guides don't compel anyone to change against their will.

While they can inspire and guide, the transformation and growth of others are choices these individuals must make for themselves.

Overriding karmic lessons

Spirit guides respect the karmic lessons, which are the life lessons that individuals need to learn in order to evolve spiritually.

They can advise you to overcome challenges, but they must keep the impact of karmic influences intact.

This means that they can't completely remove the challenges from your life, but they can help you navigate them with more ease and understanding.

Finding your dream partner

Your guides help you implement changes to become ready for love relationships that align with your personal and spiritual growth.

However, they can't actively find your dream spouse for you. That involves efforts of free will and the mutual compatibility of both individuals.

What can happen is that they lead you to meet someone whom you're destined to meet. But it remains up to you to decide what role you want that person to play in your life.

3.
Who Are These Spirit Guides?

This guide focuses on contact with **high-level spirit guides**, who are multidimensional beings of light and love.

Some have incarnated on Earth and ascended to higher realms. Others have never incarnated, and some of those are from other dimensions.

Terms like "spirit world" or "higher realms" describe the subtle realities where spirit guides exist. However, these terms imply a separate world or realm from our physical world, which can be misleading.

All of us are present in the spirit world as much as in the physical world. Both of these "worlds" are one. There is no separation.

The spirit world is all around us and encompassing us. It simply exists on different vibrations and frequencies.

I prefer the Vedantic and Yogic explanations of distinguishing between different sets of frequencies: the physical plane, the astral plane, the causal plane, and that which is "beyond the beyond."

1. The **physical plane** is our human reality, everything we can perceive with our five physical senses.

2. The **astral plane** consists of energy rather than physical matter. It's where most of our souls go after death before reincarnating again, and it's the home of many other types of spirit entities.

3. The **causal plane** is the most subtle, consisting only of thoughts and ideas. It's an ultra-high vibration

dimension. Very advanced spirit beings of the highest frequencies exist in this plane.

The causal plane and the "beyond the beyond" are also called multidimensional reality.

Beings from the causal plane are pure entities of love and light. They don't have physical bodies, only causal bodies made of thought. However, they may show themselves in a human body to you.

"High-level spirit guides" refers only to these highest- frequency spirit entities from the causal plane and beyond.

Time and space do not exist for them like in our earthly incarnations. They purely and lovingly reside in the Oneness of Divine Creation.

There are different types of high-level spirit guides from the causal plane and beyond:

Deities

Deities are divine entities with unique qualities and attributes. In Hinduism, for example, deities like Vishnu, Shiva, and Lakshmi represent aspects of creation, preservation, and abundance.

Similarly, in Greek mythology, gods and goddesses like Athena, Zeus, and Aphrodite embody wisdom, supreme authority, and love.

As spirit guides, deities connect the physical and causal planes. Establishing a relationship with a deity can provide holy guidance, protection, wisdom, and much more.

The notion of deities as spirit guides has evolved beyond traditional religious frameworks of birth.

You're free to draw eclectic inspiration from different pantheons and belief systems, creating a personalized synthesis that resonates with your soul. Or you can choose to stick to one or none of the belief systems. All of these options are okay and have no impact on the quality of your spirit communication.

When you apply the "Ten-Step Method" to communicate with your spirit guides, a deity may or may not appear. Accept whoever comes through as long as it is a high-frequency being from the causal plane. Don't be disappointed if it is not a deity that connects with you.

Guardian Angels

Across various cultures, the concept of guardian angels as spirit guides transcends religious boundaries.

As personal guardians, they accompany us from birth to death, offering protection, guidance, and assistance during times of need.

In moments of danger, crisis, or challenges, your guardian angel is a vigilant protector, shielding you from harm and ensuring your well-being. Your guardian angel knows you inside out and is happy to offer you spiritual direction and insight.

Your guardian angel has always communicated with you through subtle signs, intuitive feelings, and synchronicities, guiding you toward positive choices for your higher spiritual good.

You can actively start talking with your guardian angel with the "Ten-Step Method." All humans have a guardian angel in their family of spirit guides, and some have more than one.

Archangels and other Angels

Archangels, often considered the highest order of angels, play unique roles in facilitating communication between the divine and the human dimensions. Each of them possesses specific responsibilities.

For example, Michael offers protection and courage, Raphael can support you with his healing abilities, Gabriel with communication, and Uriel with wisdom.

As spirit guides, archangels offer incredibly precious guidance and support in specific areas of life. They work tirelessly to support your spiritual growth. Their guidance extends from immediate challenges to broader soul lessons and pursuing higher virtues.

Other types of angels may be in your spirit guide family, each with a unique role. They differ by their element (for example, water angels, fire angels, etc.) or their role in specific religions (for instance, Cherubim in Christianity or Malakim in Judaism).

Communicating directly with archangels and other angels will provide protection, guidance, wisdom, and strength to navigate life's complexities with grace and resilience.

In your spirit communication with angels, you may experience profound insights, like feeling an overwhelming sense of peace and gratitude or receiving very clear and actionable guidance.

Ascended Masters

Ascended masters are highly evolved spiritual beings who once walked the Earth as humans. They have achieved a much higher level of consciousness and ascended to a state of spiritual Enlightenment without needing earthly reincarnations anymore.

Each Ascended Master has specific qualities, teachings, and areas of expertise. These are well-known examples of Ascended Masters:

- Jesus Christ - Love, compassion, and spiritual teaching
- Mother Mary - Maternal love and divine guidance
- Padre Pio - Miracles, healing, and devotion
- Francis of Assisi - Love for nature, humility, and service
- Buddha - Compassion and path to liberation from suffering
- Saint Germain - Transformation, alchemy, spiritual initiation
- Kuthumi - Wisdom, teaching, and spiritual guidance
- Lady Nada - Divine love and healing relationships
- Serapis Bey - Ascension, purity, and spiritual discipline
- White Buffalo Calf Woman - Prophecy, peace, and ceremonies

When applying the "Ten-Step Method" to communicate with your spirit guides, you might encounter one of these extraordinary beings or one of the many other Ascended Masters who are lesser known.

Ascended Spirit Animals

Spirit animals are worshiped as guides and companions in indigenous cultures and shamanic traditions.

Ascended spirit animals possess a spiritual consciousness that transcends their previous physical existence. They have evolved to a high-frequency state similar to the enlightened state of ascended masters.

Each ascended spirit animal is associated with particular symbolism and archetypal qualities. For example, an eagle symbolizes vision, freedom, and spiritual insight, while a wolf represents intuition, loyalty, and social connection.

Honoring the spiritual essence of animals fosters a deeper connection to nature and all living beings. You may encounter one or several ascended spirit animals when applying the "Ten-Step Method." They may also talk to you in dreams or appear to you as messengers in a physical shape.

Ascended Ancestors

Similar to ascended masters, some of your ancestors may have reached Enlightenment and ascended to the causal plane.

They care about and deeply connect with you as you're in their family. They're guardians of the family lineage with a vested interest in the well-being and prosperity of their descendants.

Ancestral worship is a longstanding tradition in many cultures where the wisdom and contributions of past generations are acknowledged and revered.

Ascended ancestors can choose to serve as spirit guides, offering guidance, protection, and support to their living relatives.

Their wisdom encompasses practical advice for navigating challenges as well as insights into cultural and spiritual traditions and the values that define your family heritage.

3. Who Are These Spirit Guides?

Their guidance may also extend to addressing and healing ancestral trauma and other unresolved issues within your family.

By acknowledging and working through these challenges, you can contribute to the healing and collective evolution of all your living family members with the support of your ancestors.

Ethereal Beings Who Have Never Incarnated

Diverse beings who haven't gone through earthly incarnations exist in the causal plane and beyond. These high-frequency entities, free from the constraints of material existence, possess profound wisdom, heightened awareness, and a deep understanding of universal truths.

You may encounter such ethereal beings and talk to them when applying the "Ten-Step Method." They can also communicate with you through dreams, symbols, visions, subtle energetic conduits, intuition, and intrinsic knowing.

Guides From The Astral Plane

Various beings from the astral plane can serve as spirit guides, too, such as ancestors and spirit animals, deceased loved ones and pets, nature spirits, etc.

You can also apply the "Ten-Step Method" to talk to astral plane guides.

However, many lesser types of spiritual entities also inhibit the astral plane. You'll find more information about distinguishing and dealing with lower-vibration entities In Chapter 8.

This book only focuses on communication with high-level spirit guides from the causal plane and beyond to ensure maximum benefit and safety for you.

Please never apply this method for "voodoo"-type practices trying to contact lowest-level spirit entities.

Spirit Guides Can Appear In Many Forms

Spirit guides can appear in many forms tailored to our needs and receptivity.

When applying the "Ten-Step Method" to consciously connect with them, you can perceive their presence in multiple ways.

Some sense them through physical sensations like tingling, energy movements, or a comforting encompassing energy, often accompanied by warmth in one or several chakras.

Some can hear their soothing voices talking or singing. Some can see a color, sign, symbol, image, face, entire body, or even a full-fledged apparition. Others can smell them, taste them, or become intuitively and knowingly aware of their loving energy.

For most of us, spirit communication flows through a combination of these "clairsenses," explained in more detail in the next chapter.

Spirit guides from the causal plane can freely choose in which form they appear to us. They adjust their form to how you can best perceive them. They can utilize a male or a female form, although they don't have a gender. Some prefer not to appear in any form.

Ascended masters, ancestors, and spirit animals may use a form from their last or previous incarnations.

As you practice the "Ten-Step Method" to consciously connect with your guides, you'll become more accustomed to perceiving their presence, and they will appear to you more clearly. You'll immediately recognize its energy after repeatedly talking to the same guide.

These are AI-rendered examples of how my three spirit guides described in the introduction appear to me:

El Cateño

Sanskinani

Niaku

More About High-Level Guides From The Causal Plane

Polarity, time, and space do not exist for beings from the causal plane like for humans on the physical plane.

That's why they have endless patience with you. They're never in a hurry like we sometimes are, but they fully understand the concept of time and space and how we are bound to it.

These high-vibrational beings cannot feel negative emotions like sadness, fear, guilt, envy, or shame. They are pure love and compassion.

They can't be angry at you, and they'll never be disappointed with you. They admire us for experiencing the entire range of feelings on our physical plane.

High-level spirit guides must adjust their frequencies to communicate with us. It becomes easier for them to talk to you when you raise your frequency. You can use the meditation presented in Chapter 10 and all the information in Chapter 14 for that purpose.

Their high-frequency state allows them to communicate with various spiritual and physical entities in parallel. Thus, one high-level spirit guide can simultaneously serve thousands or even millions of human souls.

They can see and cause things that our minds cannot comprehend.

They have access to any information they need through the Akashic records. They know everything about us, everything we have ever experienced, done, said, or thought, even our most private reflections and beliefs.

However, they can't and would never judge you for anything you think or do. They're totally free of any judgment. So, in their presence, you can free yourself of any guilt or shame you feel about your past.

They know exactly how difficult it is to incorporate on planet Earth, and they marvel at your soul for having made that choice.

No high-level spirit guide can ever interfere with your free will. We're free to influence our present and future through our thoughts and actions.

That's why your spirit guides don't make future predictions. They can't foresee our individual and collective acts of free will. They'll tell you what can happen and explain the likely consequences of your decisions, but they can't tell you what will undoubtedly occur.

How Many Spirit Guides Do We Have?

Just like high-level spirit guides can support thousands of human beings, your mind and soul can also connect to several spirit guides.

Each human being gets support from an entire team of high-level spiritual entities, your "family" of spirit guides.

Even at the highest levels, they have different talents and areas of expertise. Your spirit guide family combines a unique mix of skills and experience to support you in the best possible way.

Some spirit guides are with you for your lifetime, while others only come for a certain period. There is no fixed number or maximum of guides in your spirit family.

4.
How Do Your Spirit Guides Talk To You?

High-level spirit guides talk to us and send us messages in various ways. For example, when you have a strong gut feeling or suddenly see an image or a symbol in your mind, a spirit guide is likely talking to you.

They're sending us information similar to radio waves. It's just a matter of learning how to increase your frequency and connect with your high-level guides to tune in and listen.

Applying the "Ten-Step Method" for direct communication with your guides facilitates adjusting the frequencies and allows you to receive their messages more clearly.

You'll use one or several of your "clairsenses" to interpret what they're broadcasting:

Clairvoyance (clear seeing)

Clairvoyance, derived from the French words "clair" (clear) and "voyance" (vision), means seeing visions of images, symbols, clips, or entire movies through your mind's eye.

One fascinating aspect of clairvoyance is its diverse range of expressions. Some of us see symbolic representations that require interpretation, while others experience lucid visions with intricate details.

Your spirit guides may send you images and symbols and take you on complete visual journeys.

Clairaudience (clear hearing)

Clairaudience is the intuitive ability to receive auditory information. It lets you hear voices, sounds, and messages that don't have a source in the physical realm.

Spirit guides may speak to you in subtle whispers, gentle words, distinct voices, genuine slang, or symbolic sounds. They may also sing or play music for you.

You've probably experienced an old song suddenly playing in your head, which could be a message from one of your guides, but it could also be your brain bringing it up from memory.

Reflect on the essence of everything you hear from your guides.

Clairsentience (clear feeling)

Clairsentience means picking up emotions, energies, and vibrations beyond our physical sensory perception.

You've probably intuitively sensed the feelings of others around you or grasped the atmospheres of different spaces.

Spirit guides can harness the language of clairsentience to show their presence via physical experiences like tingling sensations or changes in temperature in your hands, feet, chakras, or other body parts.

Moreover, they can induce an emotion you'll feel as part of a message. Meditating on that emotion can tell you more about its significance in your life and what's underneath it.

Clairfragrance (clear smelling)

Clairfragrance, or clairalience, involves the ability to smell scents or odors not present in the physical environment.

You may experience the smell of flowers, distinct fragrances, or other scents associated with physical or spiritual energies.

The odors encountered through clairalience can carry symbolic meanings and convey messages from your guides, adding a dimension of sensory richness to your intuitive experience.

By infusing the environment with specific scents or fragrances, spirit guides create a unique language that may trigger memories, evoke emotions, or serve as distinct markers of their presence.

Consider what a scent means to you and what it reminds you of when you perceive it in your spirit communication.

Clairgustance (clear tasting)

Clairgustance involves tasting flavors and sensations without any physical stimulus. These tastes can be subtle or intense, ranging from sweetness to bitterness, and may carry symbolic significance.

Clairgustance adds a unique and flavorful aspect to the spectrum of extrasensory perception.

Reflect on a taste's attributes and what it means to you if you experience clairgustance when talking to your spirit guides.

Claircognizance (clear knowing)

Claircognizance, or clear knowing, is an intuitive ability to "just know something clearly" and perceive it with a strong sense of certainty and conviction.

You may receive insights, ideas, solutions, or a sudden, unshakable understanding of a situation or person.

Your spirit guides import guidance and answers to your questions directly into your consciousness, bypassing the need for explicit language or symbolic messages.

All of us have abilities in some or all clairsenses. For most, one or two of these senses are dominant. Your spirit guides will adjust to your abilities to receive and interpret their information.

They'll fine-tune their messages to you and your dominant senses so you can better understand them.

Besides directly talking to you through your clairsenses in active communication sessions, your spirit guides also have many indirect ways of sending you messages:

Dreams

Dream communication allows spirit guides to bypass the rational mind, reaching the deeper layers of the subconscious and our soul. They may appear to you in your dreams or communicate to you through the story of a dream.

Try to be aware of your dreams, especially the most vivid ones, and reflect on what they mean to you. Some dreams may include profound insights, guidance, or gentle nudges toward specific actions or decisions.

However, not every dream comes from a spirit guide. Some are simply processes of your subconscious mind.

Signs and Symbols

Spirit guides like to communicate through signs and symbols, offering a subtle yet profound language.

Such signs can appear in everyday experiences, such as repeated patterns, encounters with specific animals, or meaningful coincidences.

Signs can also manifest in nature, such as the weather, patterns in clouds, or the appearance of particular plants and stones.

Meditate on what a sign or symbol you receive and its context and colors mean to you.

Animal and Plant Messengers

Spirit guides can send us animal and plant messengers, especially when they know we associate a special meaning with that animal or plant.

Look up and be attentive to the natural environment around you. Animals are your spiritual allies, each carrying unique energies and symbolism.

Plants can also serve as messengers, with their energy and characteristics holding symbolic meaning.

A blooming flower might signal personal blossoming, while a sturdy tree embodies strength and resilience. Animals and plants can appear in dreams and daily life. They can carry messages or simply share their characteristics with us.

Connect to animal and plant messengers and use your intuition to unveil their guidance. What do they stand for? What are they telling you about their movement and their being?

Songs and Music

Spirit guides like to communicate through songs and music, too. You might hear a songline repeatedly or at meaningful moments playing in your head, on the radio, or elsewhere. Lyrics, melodies, and the timing of a musical appearance can hold symbolic meaning.

Pay attention to the lyrics, emotional resonance, and context in which the music appears to better understand what it means to you.

Crystals

Every crystal carries a unique vibration, and most can act as a conduit for messages from your guides.

You may intuitively find yourself drawn to a specific crystal, or one may somehow appear in your life.

Working with crystals can support the "Ten-Step Method" practice to create a strong channel for receiving guidance, as the crystal's energy connects with your spiritual frequency and acts as a bridge to support talking to high-level spirit guides.

The choice of crystals varies depending on your situation and personal preferences. For example, amethyst signifies spiritual growth and protection, while rose quartz conveys love, healing, and cleansing.

Clear quartz crystals are the best choice to support your spirit communication. Their transparency and purity allow for a clear channel to high-frequency spiritual entities, and they can amplify spiritual energy.

You can hold a clear quartz crystal in meditation and spirit communication sessions.

Genuine "Lemurian" quartz crystals are extra powerful and highly recommended. They're strong companions to help us cleanse and focus our energy and enhance our empathy, communication, and psychic abilities.

If you can get your hands on a Lemurian crystal with a "channeler" or even a "dow" formation, go for it if you can afford it!

A "channeler" 7-3 crystal has seven sides on its main face and three on the opposite face.

A "dow" crystal has a perfect 7-3-7-3-7-3 sides formation over all six faces.

Synchronicities

Synchronicities are meaningful coincidences that are not causally related but have a significant connection or resonance.

High-level spirit guides love arranging synchronicities in your life. They can align external events and navigate us toward them at the right moment. They also like leading us to meet people who can teach and inspire us.

Stay connected with your guides, and be open and aware of strong intuitions and gut feelings. Dare to act on them to experience more guided synchronicities in your life.

Numbers

Another way spirit guides communicate to us is through numbers or number sequences. They may arrange for you to repeatedly encounter specific numbers in various contexts, such as license plates, phone numbers, or addresses. The repetition is a deliberate attempt to draw your attention.

A particular number or sequence may hold personal significance to you. Reflect on that when a number comes up repeatedly, and you can read up on its numerology and spiritual meaning.

Sudden Guidance

Sudden guidance from spirit guides can occur outside of direct and conscious spirit communication sessions.

It may manifest as immediate clear insights or ideas, a solid inner knowing, a feeling of certainty, or a subtle nudge.

Sudden strong gut feelings may warn you of danger or lead you toward a positive new experience or encounter. Trust your intuition and gut feelings, and always be aware and open to receiving them.

Weird Occurrences

Spirit guides sometimes communicate through unexpected occurrences in the physical world that many people would consider weird or spooky.

For example, they may surprise you with lights or electrical devices that suddenly turn on or off.

You may also experience books falling off the shelves or other objects moving.

You might suddenly find objects that you can't explain where they come from, like white feathers.

Such occurrences can be signs from your guides that may contain a message and express their desire to connect and communicate with you.

Be aware of your your surroundings. Reflect on the timing and context when "weird" occurrences happen to you. For example, it's no coincidence which book is falling off the shelf or what a switched-on light is shining upon.

The best way to clarify what subtle indirect messages genuinely mean is to ask your guides in an active spirit communication session using the "Ten-Step Method."

5.
When Should You Talk to Your Guides?

Your spirit guides constantly talk to you, and you can connect to talk to them actively **anytime**.

When you wish to commit to regular active spirit communication using the "Ten-Step Method," it's a good idea to set a **regular date** for your sessions.

Your spirit guides offer you a wonderful relationship of unconditional love and support. So why not show them you take this relationship seriously by allocating your time for regular meetings?

Depending on your available time, it can be a daily date or once or twice a week. The regularity demonstrates your commitment to your guides and your practice, and it helps you to go deeper in every session.

Once you have set a regular date with your guides, it matters that you actually show up. Like with human beings, it's about respecting them and yourself.

Show them that you take the connection and communication with them seriously, but don't beat yourself up if you can't make it on a given day. Just show up again the next time.

How much time does spirit communication take?

A spirit communication session can last anywhere from five minutes to several hours. You're in control. You decide how much time you want to invest.

A quick session can be helpful to get urgently needed advice or a fast reply, while extended and open-ended sessions allow you to explore deep topics with your guides and let them take you on journeys via your clairsenses.

You should schedule about an hour each for your regular sessions, if possible. That will give you enough time to complete the ten steps thoroughly and talk to your guides without haste.

Even though the concept of time does not apply to your high-level guides, they are well aware of when you're in a hurry, and they'll fine-tune their messages accordingly to give you the information you need in the time available.

What's the best time for spirit communication?

These daytimes are considered best for meditation and spirit communication:

Morning (around 6 AM or earlier)

For many, early morning is the best time to talk to their spirit guides. During these early hours, before work and other commitments start competing for your attention, you have the focus and clarity to fully engage in your practice.

An early morning practice allows you to set your intention for the day, explore any questions, and receive guidance from your wonderful friends. If you don't have time for an entire session, just go for a quick reconnection (see Chapter 13).

Lunchtime (around noon)

If morning and evening sessions don't fit your routine, you may consider scheduling your spirit communication during your lunch break. Even if you have only 20 or 30 minutes, you can use them to connect with your spirit guides and angels.

Evening (around 6 PM or later)

Evening spirit communication sessions are the second best option after mornings. When your primary daily duties and chores are complete, you can relax and focus on the unique gift of talking to your spirit guide family.

Spirit communication is much more accessible on an empty stomach. When our body is busy digesting, it has less energy and clarity available for anything else. Don't schedule your dates with your guides right after a meal. Eating after your sessions is better.

Physical exercise before your spirit communication sessions can be of great benefit, as it purifies and relaxes your body. Doing yoga, going to the gym, or engaging in any other physical activity you prefer is an excellent preparation for your practice.

The best time for your spirit guide dates depends on your preference and lifestyle. Choose a time that aligns with your natural rhythm and allows for inner stillness and calmness.

6.
Where Can You Talk to Your Spirit Guides?

You can communicate with your guides from **anywhere**, and they can send you messages wherever you are.

Of course, talking to your guides is hard when you're in a noisy place full of people.

It's much easier to have your spirit communication session where you can enjoy some time of undisturbed privacy. If there does happen to be some noise, you can integrate it into your experience without bothering about it.

Creating a **sacred space** for your regular dates with your spirit guides is highly recommended. It can be in your home or your garden. It can also be your favorite place in nature.

Mountains, rivers, lakes, and beaches are especially suitable for that. But it's **your** sacred space. Choose it freely anywhere you like.

If your sacred space is in your home, you may want to use a meditation cushion and create an altar. Feel free to decorate it as you wish.

You can use statues and images of any deities you believe in, crystals, plants, flowers, candles, incense, photographs of loved ones or special places, and other items that are sacred to you.

The more sessions with your guides you'll have in your sacred space, the easier it'll become to connect to them. Practicing at a regular time and place stores energy patterns in that location that benefit and enhance your practice.

7.
What Can You Ask Your Spirit Guides?

You can ask your high-level spirit guides anything you want once you have established a strong connection with them using the "Ten-Step Method."

They're more than happy to give you their replies and deep insights into open questions such as:

- "What matters most for me right now?"
- "What message do you have for me today?"
- "What is my situation in life? What direction should I take?"
- "What is the most important lesson I need to learn right now?"
- "What is my soul's plan, and how can I fully align with it?"
- "How can I release my emotional blockages?"
- "What actions can I take to manifest my dreams?"
- "What can I do to attract abundance and prosperity?"
- "How can I overcome ... (situation)?"
- "What decision should I make regarding ... (situation)?"
- "What do I need to consider for... (situation)?"
- "What is the truth about ... (person/situation)?"
- "How can I improve my relationship with ... (person)?"
- "How can I overcome ... (challenge/situation)?"
- "How can I achieve ... (personal goal)?
- "Where should I go, and how can I benefit from it (journey)?

You can also use yes or no questions. However, your guides can't answer every question with a yes or no. They typically like to show you both sides, the consequences of a yes and a no.

You can literally ask your guides anything, from very practical or seemingly irrelevant mundane questions to relationship queries or deep, fundamental spiritual inquiries.

As you already know, they never make future predictions, so don't ask for that. But they'll tell you what to consider for your decisions and the most likely consequences. They can also inspire you about which actions you can take right now that will likely improve your future.

They won't tell you who your next lover or dream spouse is. But they'll highlight truths about the people in your life and show you how to attract the right partner.

They won't tell you how to get rich quickly. But they'll let you know what steps you can take to tap into prosperity and abundance.

Spirit guides will **immediately** reply to your questions. When they're in full connection with you, they may elaborate further on the question or even take you on a journey to give you further insights into it.

Initially, you may be unable to establish a complete connection with your guides or decipher and understand all of their replies. Don't despair if that happens. Try again another day. The more you practice this type of communication, the easier it will become.

8.
How to Ensure Safety?

Safety is a top priority in spirit communication.

Following the "Ten-Step Method" precisely as described in Chapter 11 guarantees that you'll always be 100% safe when communicating with your spirit guide family.

The method ensures you communicate exclusively with loving high-level spirit guides from the causal plane, where no less-evolved spiritual entities exist.

According to the spiritual laws, no spirit entity can break your free will. Beings in the spirit world cannot interfere with whatever we choose to do on our physical plane.

Therefore, **communication with spirit guides can only happen if you consciously allow it and with whom you permit it**.

You are in complete control at any time during your spirit communication sessions. All spiritual entities can only speak to you with your permission.

Ask for a high-level guide, and one will be there.

If you wish to end the communication, you may do so anytime.

How To Recognize High-Level Spirit Guides

Connecting with a high-level spirit guide always feels warm, comfortable, loving, uplifting, inspiring, and wonderful.

High-level guides come to shine a light on your path. Their only wish is for your higher good. They'll never frighten you nor build up your ego. They won't flatter you, but they may applaud your success.

High-level guides express themselves precisely and say a lot in a few words or images. They speak only in good terms about the people and situations in your life because they are full of love.

They want us to use our discernment rather than mindlessly follow what we're told. They'll never impose on you that you must do something specific.

They'll never attempt to influence your life choices and your free will. High-level guides lead you toward having greater confidence in your own truth.

Use your common sense to evaluate if the information you receive from them rings true to you. Listen to your heart and only follow their advice if it feels right.

How To Recognize Entities Who Are Less Evolved

If you follow the "Ten-Step Method," connections with less-evolved spiritual entities will not happen during your spirit communication sessions.

But you should know how to recognize and deal with such beings in case one of them ever tries to connect with you.

There are indeed less-evolved entities in the astral plane. Some are "lost souls" who desire to return to Earth and experience life through you. There are also many other types of entities on the lower levels of the astral plane.

Most don't have an evil intent; they just seek attention. Similar to humans on the physical plane, they range from friendly, to occasionally helpful, to playful, to neutral, to naughty, to malicious.

They may appear in a wide variety of imaginary forms. Most of them are harmless and will only try to waste your time.

You'll immediately know and feel that something is wrong if you connect with such a lower-level spiritual entity. Communication with these beings does not feel good.

They may seem heavy and stir up confusing or negative emotions. You'll recognize their lack of peace, fear, pain, or uncertainty. You may feel worried, anxious, scared, or powerless when in contact with them.

Spirit entities will not deceive you if you ask them who they are and where they are from.

If you ask them if they are from the light, they cannot answer with a "yes" if they are not.

Ask them to show you their true nature if you're not sure what kind of entity you are connected to.

As you communicate more often with your family of high-level spirit guides, you'll know exactly how each of them feels. It'll become impossible for another being to fool you.

What To Do If You're In Contact With A Less-Evolved Entity

If any entities other than high-level loving guides from the causal plane ever try to connect with you and you feel discomfort, immediately tell them "no" firmly and clearly.

Ask the entity to leave and tell it to go to the light. Say that out loud, clearly, and firmly, then end the communication.

Be firm and sever the link. You can visualize cutting all energy chords between you and that entity.

Come back to the present moment and open your eyes. Take a few deep breaths and drink a glass of water.

Then, ground yourself again, as described in the next Chapter. Don't attempt another spirit guide connection immediately.

You can perform a cleansing ritual to clear the negative energy, such as smudging with sage or any other method described in Chapter 12 under "Clear Negative Energy."

If you feel that the same less-evolved entity repeatedly tries to connect with you against your will, ask Archangel Michael for help and protection.

Consciously ask Michael at the beginning of every meditation and spirit communication session to wrap his purple light cocoon of protection around you.

Also, ask him to use his sword to cut any ties between that entity and you.

Depending on your religion and belief system, you may ask a deity like Shiva or Buddha for help and protection instead of Archangel Michael.

9.
Powerful Grounding Meditation

The following grounding meditation is crucial in the "Ten-Step Method to Spirit Communication."

However, you can also do this meditation independently of talking to your spirit guides whenever you feel scattered, anxious, overwhelmed, scared, depressed, or disconnected.

Regular grounding helps you feel more centered, balanced, and connected to the present moment, your body, and Mother Earth. It fosters a sense of inner peace and stability amidst life's challenges.

Grounding before engaging in spirit communication is essential for maintaining focus, protection, and clarity. It creates an energetic boundary that helps filter out distractions.

Furthermore, grounding improves your emotional stability, which can be helpful for effectively interpreting the messages you receive from your guides.

It also helps to regulate the energy flow in your body, preventing you from feeling drained or overwhelmed during your sessions.

Grounding is a foundational practice and the best preparation for safe, clear, and respectful interactions with your spirit guides.

Follow these steps for your powerful grounding meditation:

Step 1:

Sit comfortably in a quiet space where you won't be disturbed, ideally in your "sacred space," as described in Chapter 6. You can sit on a meditation cushion or a chair. Don't lie down.

Try to keep your back straight if possible. However, if that's painful for you or requires a special effort, just sit comfortably!

Step 2:

Close your eyes and take several slow, deep breaths. Inhale profoundly into your stomach, filling it with air from the bottom like a vase fills with water.

When exhaling, let go of the air effortlessly and reversely, from top to bottom. Feel the breath entering and leaving your body, allowing yourself to relax with each exhale.

Keep focusing your attention on how you slowly breathe in and out. If thoughts interfere, let them go again and return to the present moment.

Step 3:

Picture yourself surrounded by a warm, bright light filled with golden sparkles. Inhale this beautiful light with every breath.

Inhale the bright light with golden sparkles around you

Bring your attention to your body and become aware of any tension or discomfort you may be holding. Starting from your feet, gradually scan your body.

Keep inhaling the golden light, and release any stress, tension, or negativity into the ground with every exhale, allowing it to be absorbed and transmuted.

Take as many deep breaths as you like until you have scanned your entire body and feel tranquil, relaxed, and comfortable.

Step 4:

Stay with your deep breaths and focus on the space between your anus and your genitals, also called your pelvic floor or perineum.

Exhale intensely into this space. It's your root chakra. Visualize how it gets activated in its dark red color.

You might notice how it gets warmer while focusing on and breathing into it.

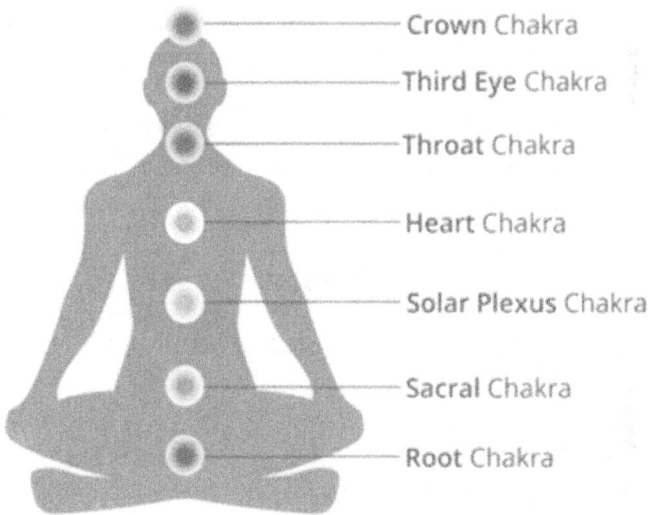

Crown Chakra
Third Eye Chakra
Throat Chakra
Heart Chakra
Solar Plexus Chakra
Sacral Chakra
Root Chakra

Location of the root chakra and your other chakras

Step 5:

Start visualizing an energy chord, a vortex that extends from your root chakra deep into the Earth, growing like a root but much faster.

Exhale into this vortex with every breath, strengthen it, and make it extend deeper into the Earth.

Take your time and keep breathing into your energy chord. Visualize and feel how it gets more robust and profound with every exhale.

As you keep breathing into it, your energy chord expands further and further into the ground. Perhaps you can already feel it extending all the way to the center of the Earth.

Picture the Earth's center as a granite ball or as a ball of fire. While still breathing into it, visualize wrapping your energy chord around this ball and fastening it thoroughly.

Take as much time as you need to extend and attach your energy chord firmly to the Earth's center. Take a few deep breaths and observe your state after you've completed that.

Step 6:

Your energy chord is now solidly anchored at the Earth's center.

Visualize and feel how a soothing, nurturing energy slowly rises back up from the Earth, merging with the golden light around you.

Inhale the golden light and the nurturing Earth energy with every breath through the top of your head, your crown chakra, while still exhaling into your energy chord.

Keep breathing in this energetic cycle for as long as you like. Feel how your inclusion into the Earth's energy cycle and exchange comforts you.

Step 7:

Express gratitude for Mother Earth's support and the grounding energy you have received. Feel a sense of appreciation for the natural world around you.

When you're ready, gently bring your awareness back to the present moment. Wiggle your fingers and toes, stretch your body, and open your eyes.

10.
Raising Your Frequency Meditation

Raising your frequency or vibrational energy facilitates spirit communication tremendously.

Your high-level spirit guides from the causal plane vibrate on a very high frequency, much higher than any human being.

Raising your frequency makes it easier for them to adjust to it and clearly convey their messages to you.

Increasing your frequency with this meditation can also positively affect your quality of life in these areas:

- **Mental clarity and focus**: You may notice a significant improvement in your ability to concentrate, solve problems creatively, and maintain a clear, alert mind throughout your day.

- **Emotional Resilience**: You become better equipped to navigate life's ups and downs by aligning with higher vibrational energies. Challenges may seem less overwhelming, and you'll be more adept at managing stress and negative emotions.

- **Physical Health**: A higher frequency supports your body's natural ability to maintain balance, which leads to enhanced energy levels, strengthened immune function, and better overall well-being.

- **Spiritual Connection**: You may experience deep moments of insight, intuition, spiritual awakening, and a sense of connection with everything that exists in the present moment by increasing your frequency.

- **Positive Experiences:** Higher vibrational energies act as magnets for positive experiences, people, and opportunities. You draw love, abundance, and happiness into your life by raising your frequency.

- **Personal Growth:** When consciously choosing higher vibrational thoughts, emotions, and actions, you catalyze shifts in consciousness that ripple outwards into every aspect of your life, resulting in personal growth and transformation.

- **Authentic Self:** You create space for your true essence to shine through as you shed lower vibrational energies like fear, doubt, and self-limiting beliefs.

Like the grounding meditation, the meditation to raise your frequency is an essential step in the "Ten-Step Method."

You can also do it independently of your spirit communication, and you'll get the best results if you do both meditations in sequence, first grounding and then raising your frequency.

The first three steps are the same in both meditations. You can skip these steps in the second meditation if you do both meditations in sequence. Otherwise, proceed from the beginning:

Step 1:

Sit comfortably in a quiet space where you won't be disturbed, ideally in your "sacred space," as described in Chapter 6. You can sit on a meditation cushion or a chair. Don't lie down.

Try to keep your back straight if possible. However, if that's painful for you or requires a special effort, just sit comfortably!

Step 2:

Close your eyes and take several slow, deep breaths. Inhale profoundly into your stomach, filling it with air from the bottom like a vase fills with water.

When exhaling, let go of the air effortlessly and reversely, from top to bottom. Feel the breath entering and leaving your body, allowing yourself to relax with each exhale.

Keep focusing your attention on how you slowly breathe in and out. If thoughts interfere, let them go again and return to the present moment.

Step 3:

Picture yourself surrounded by a warm, bright light filled with golden sparkles. Inhale this beautiful light with every breath.

Bring your attention to your body and become aware of any tension or discomfort you may be holding. Starting from your feet, gradually scan your body.

Keep inhaling the golden light, and release any stress, tension, or negativity into the ground with every exhale, allowing it to be absorbed and transmuted.

Take as many deep breaths as you like until you have scanned your entire body and feel tranquil, relaxed, and comfortable.

Step 4:

Focus your attention on your heart chakra, which is in the center of your chest, next to your physical heart.

Breathe into your heart chakra with every exhale while still inhaling the golden light.

Feel how it activates and opens up more and more with every breath.

Step 5:

Start expanding your aura, your energy field, outwards from your heart chakra while exhaling into it.

Visualize how it extends further and further with every breath in all directions. You may feel it growing far beyond your body and location.

Sense how your heart connects with every living being in your expanded energy field, how you become one with all that exists.

Keep breathing into it and growing it for as long as you like. You may feel a deep sense of peace and unity in your heart.

Step 6:

Bring your attention back to your body and focus on the crown chakra on top of your head. Breathe into it like you have done with the heart chakra in the last step.

Feel how it gets activated and opens up toward the sky.

You are now going on a journey, allowing your consciousness to rise through your crown chakra into space.

Picture a crystal light bubble that contains your consciousness and rises slowly and effortlessly. You feel safe and serene in that bubble.

Your crystal bubble might look similar to this one.
Visualize it in any way you like!

Move up in your bubble through the clouds into the sky. With each breath, you rise higher into the universe. You can see beautiful stars sparkling around you. You feel calm and serene.

Keep breathing deeply and become aware of how your vibration rises along with the higher heights you are reaching.

You ascend further and further up, higher and higher, across stars and galaxies, possibly all the way to the edge of the ever-expanding Universe.

Observe and become aware of the subtle energies you are experiencing now. You might feel a Divine light or energy embracing you in this safe and sacred space.

Take a few more breaths and stay there as long as you like.

Step 7:

Gradually bring your attention back to your physical body.

Express gratitude for the love in your heart power and the high vibration you have experienced.

When you feel ready, gently come back to the present moment. Wiggle your fingers and toes, stretch your body, and open your eyes.

11.
Ten-Step Method To Spirit Communication

Most resources about spirit communication inform you about ways your spirit guides talk to you, similar to the descriptions in Chapter 4.

However, they usually don't give clear step-by-step instructions on initiating an active connection and communication session with your spirit guides to seek their guidance and support.

I have practiced and fine-tuned the "Ten-Step Method" presented in this Chapter for over 25 years for all my spirit communication. It has proven to work very well for many beginners and more advanced practitioners to whom I have introduced it.

Follow the walkthrough to practice, and read the explanations for each step. Anyone can learn these ten steps. All you need is a bit of time and dedication. Practice it a few times and see how it works for you.

I advise you to complete all the steps. Don't skip anything. The complete sequence of grounding yourself, opening your heart, raising your vibration, and allowing your spirit guide into your energy field is crucial to facilitating connection and communication with your guide. If you don't have enough time, go only for a quick reconnection (see Chapter 13).

Don't give up if nothing happens the first time or if what happens is not what you were hoping for. Try again another day and refer to the next chapter to overcome blockages. The most common blockage is our "monkey mind."

The more you practice, the more it'll become second nature. You'll stay connected to your guides and receive their messages even when you're not in an active session.

The first part of this Chapter contains a complete walkthrough of the ten steps to guide you through them. The second part provides additional information and explanations about each step.

If you have any questions about applying the ten steps correctly and talking to your spirit guides, feel free to join our community or contact me using the options listed in Chapter 15.

1. Ten-Step Walkthrough

Step 1: Sit Down Comfortably

Sit comfortably in a quiet area where you won't be disturbed, ideally in your "sacred space." You can sit on a meditation cushion or on a chair. Don't lie down. If possible, try to keep your back straight but not tense.

Step 2: Close Your Eyes and Breathe Deeply

Close your eyes and take several deep and slow breaths.

Inhale deeply into your stomach, filling your lungs with air from the bottom up like a vase fills with water.

Let go of the air effortlessly when exhaling, emptying your lungs from top to bottom.

Start inhaling through your crown chakra on top of your head, connecting yourself to the universal force.

Exhale through the root chakra between your anus and your genitals, connecting yourself to Mother Earth.

Take a few more of these deep breaths, inhaling and exhaling through your top and bottom chakras.

Become aware of any tension or discomfort you may be holding. Starting from your feet, gradually scan your body. Release any tension, stress, or negativity into the ground with your exhales, allowing it to be absorbed and transmuted by Mother Earth.

Gradually walk your attention upwards through your body, and with each exhale, release all tension and everything that doesn't belong to you.

Thoughts can always arise. When you become aware of getting caught up in a thought, simply let it go again and return your attention to your breath and the present moment. Keep applying this throughout the entire session.

Take a few more deep breaths and observe how you breathe in and out. You notice how your mind becomes more and more still with every breath.

Step 3: Ground Yourself

Picture yourself surrounded by a warm, bright light with many golden sparkles.

Start inhaling this beautiful light through your crown chakra. Observe how it spreads in your energy field and body while inhaling it.

Take a few more deep breaths, inhaling that wonderful bright light until you feel entirely filled with it.

Now, bring your attention back to your root chakra. Exhale intensely into it and through it into the Earth. Visualize it as a dark red power ball.

Feel how it activates and grows with every exhale. You might notice how it also warms up with your exhales, comforting your inner organs.

Now, start visualizing an energy chord that extends from your root chakra deep into the Earth, growing like a root but much faster. You can picture the chord as a vortex or as a light tube.

Exhale into this energy chord with every breath, strengthening it and allowing it to expand deeper and deeper into the Earth.

Take your time and keep breathing into your energy chord. Visualize how it gets bigger and grows deeper with each exhale.

As you keep breathing into it, your energy chord expands further and further into the ground for many miles. Perhaps you can already feel it extending all the way to the center of the Earth.

You can picture the Earth's center as a solid granite ball or a ball of fire, as you like. While still breathing into it, wrap your energy chord and fasten it thoroughly around the center of the Earth.

Take as much time as you need to extend and firmly attach your energy chord to the Earth's center.

When it's solidly anchored, take a few more deep breaths and observe your state. You might feel fully connected to Mother Earth, who holds and protects you in her arms like a baby.

Now, you can visualize and feel a soothing, nurturing energy slowly rising back up from Mother Earth, merging with the golden light around you.

Inhale this Earth energy and the golden light with every breath through your crown chakra while still exhaling into your root chakra and your anchored energy chord. Take a few more of these deep breaths.

You're now aware of how you flow in the Earth's energy cycle. We're permanently connected to this cycle as we walk, stand, sit, or lie on the surface of the Earth; we're just not always aware of it.

Keep breathing in this wonderful, energetic cycle for as long as you like. Express your gratitude to Mother Earth. Feel how its energy comforts you and observe your state.

Step 4: Raise Your Vibration

Bring your attention to your heart chakra, which is in the center of your chest, next to your physical heart. Breathe into your heart chakra with every exhale, as you did with the root chakra, while still inhaling the golden light through your crown chakra.

Feel how your heart chakra activates and opens up more and more with every breath. You can picture it in a dark green or pink color, as you prefer.

Now, visualize how your energy field, your aura, expands outwards from your heart chakra with every exhale.

Feel how it extends further and further in all directions: above you, below you, in front of you, in your back, and to all sides. You may sense it growing far beyond your body and your current location.

Keep breathing into your energy field and allow it to grow as much as you like.

Maybe you can feel how your heart connects with every living being in your expanded energy field, how you become one with all that exists in there.

Keep breathing into and growing your energy field for as long as you wish. You might feel a deep sense of peace and unity in your heart.

Slowly bring your attention back to your physical body and to your crown chakra on top of your head. Start exhaling into your crown chakra, as you did with the heart chakra.

Feel how your crown chakra activates and opens up toward the sky. You can picture it in a light purple color.

You're now ready to go on a sacred journey, allowing your consciousness to rise through your crown chakra into the sky.

Visualize a beautiful transparent crystal light bubble that contains your consciousness and rises slowly and effortlessly from your crown chakra upwards. You feel safe and serene in that bubble.

Feel how your consciousness moves up through the clouds into the sky in your crystal light bubble. With each breath you take, it rises higher and higher into space.

You might already see beautiful stars or even entire galaxies sparkling around you, and you feel calm and peaceful.

Keep breathing deeply and keep rising in your bubble.

Become aware of how your vibration rises along with the higher heights you are reaching.

You ascend further and further up, higher and higher, possibly all the way to the edge of our ever-expanding Universe.

Observe and be aware of the subtle energies you are experiencing now. You might feel a Divine light or a Divine energy embracing you in this safe and sacred space.

Take a few more deep breaths, stay there as long as you like, and observe your state.

Step 5: Ask and Allow Your Spirit Guide To Enter

Gradually bring your attention back to your physical body and keep breathing deeply.

You're now ready to ask and allow a spirit guide from light and love into your energy field. Your family of high-level spirit guides from the causal plane is waiting for this opportunity, making it 100% safe for you.

Raise your head, pointing your forehead to the sky. Slowly raise your arms and extend them at shoulder height with your palms facing upwards.

Your pose should be similar to this illustration.

Take three deep breaths in this position and feel the universal force flowing through your forehead and palms.

Then, say at least exactly these words aloud or firmly in your mind:

"I ask and allow my Divine spirit guide from Light and Love in the Causal Plane to enter my energy field."

Wait until you perceive a presence that feels good coming into your energy field.

You can lower your arms and forehead again when you feel your spirit guide entering.

Step 6: Welcome Your Spirit Guide

Allow your spirit guide to settle in your energy field. It usually takes some time for them to enter fully and to adjust to our frequency.

Trust the process and allow it to unfold. You're safe and in control. Breathe deeply and embrace the opportunity with gratitude.

Welcome your loving spirit guide when you feel its presence. You can give it a big mental hug, just say hello, or use any other way that feels right to you to welcome it.

Step 7: Talk To Your Spirit Guide

You're ready to talk to your spirit guide when you feel how it is present and has fully settled in.

Ask any questions you like! Initially, you may ask for its name, but don't despair if you don't receive one yet.

Feel free to ask any other questions. You can say them out loud or use your inner voice.

Your spirit guide always replies immediately. It may take some practice to understand their answers through your clairsenses. It's totally okay if you don't receive any replies or don't understand everything yet. In that case, just be aware of the presence and enjoy the connection.

Your spirit guide might take you on a visual journey instead of sending single replies. Just observe, trust, and let it happen. Don't worry about remembering every detail. You'll remember what matters.

Keep talking to your spirit guide for as long as you like!

Step 8: Thank Your Spirit Guide

When you are satisfied with the guidance you have received, or if you simply feel it's enough for today, thank your spirit guide and express your gratitude.

You can end the conversation by asking your spirit guide always to protect, support, and guide you.

You can say "thank you" out loud or only in your mind. You can express your gratitude using your body or in other ways.

Depending on your beliefs, you may also thank the universal force or any deity you believe in for the Divine Grace you have experienced.

Step 9: Allow Your Spirit Guide To Leave

Allow your spirit guide to leave your energy field. You can give permission out loud or mentally.

You can open your arms and raise your forehead again if you wish. Feel your spirit guide's energy slowly fading away through your crown chakra.

You can remain in meditation and contemplation of the guidance you have received.

Step 10: Ground Yourself Again and Open Your Eyes

Return to your deep breaths and bring your attention back to your energy chord connecting you to the center of the Earth.

Exhale into it again to ground yourself firmly and feel how it may have changed and intensified in the meantime. Express gratitude to Mother Earth for stabilizing, nurturing, and protecting you.

Move your fingers and toes and stretch your body as you like.

Allow yourself to return to the present moment and slowly open your eyes.

There is no hurry. Everything is okay as it is.

2. Explanations for Each Step

Step 1

You don't need to sit in a lotus, half-lotus, or any other position that you're not used to or that causes you physical pain.

But of course, feel free to do so if you're already used to it. You can also kneel on your cushion - whatever feels most comfortable!

Keeping your back straight during spirit communication contributes to a better flow of energy and a more receptive state, increasing the depth of your interactions with your spirit guides.

However, it's not mandatory. If sitting with a straight back is painful or requires too much effort, just sit comfortably. Find your best posture that allows you to feel at ease, relaxed, and focused.

Please do sit for your spirit communication sessions. Don't lie down. Your body associates lying down with rest and sleep, making it more challenging to maintain a focused and receptive state. It also limits your energy flow and diminishes your alertness.

Step 2

Simply observing your deep breaths is a powerful meditation technique by itself.

You can take as many of these initial deep breaths as you like. Breathe longer if you feel scattered or distracted, and observe how your mind becomes more still with every breath. For advanced practitioners, three deep breaths can be sufficient.

Observing your thoughts is a key practice in meditation and spirit communication.

Don't beat yourself up if you happen to get caught up in a thought. Don't go into stories about the content of a thought. Just return your attention to your breath.

Be only the observer. Notice how thoughts arise and disappear again. You can picture watching your thoughts pass by like clouds in the sky, not getting attached to them.

If you keep getting a recurring thought that bugs you, you can visualize exhaling it through your root chakra into the Earth, similar to the tensions in your body. If it comes back, exhale it again.

Step 3

This step contains the most important parts of the powerful grounding meditation. For more details, please refer to Chapter 9.

Step 4

This step contains the most important parts of the raising your vibration meditation. For more details, please refer to Chapter 10.

Step 5

Allowing your high-level spirit guides into your energy field makes it much easier for them to adjust to your frequency and convey their messages more clearly. It's 100% safe with your family of spirit guides from the causal plane.

Please use the exact words stated in the walkthrough to ask and allow your guide into your energy field. Including "Divine" and "from Light and Love" ensures that only high-level guides from the causal plane can enter your energy field. Light is more powerful than darkness, and love is the most potent force in the Universe.

They know who the perfect guide for you is right now. Ask for a Divine spirit guide, and the right one will come through. Have faith and trust in your intuition.

Don't invoke a particular guide or a deity you believe in. Let your all-knowing family from the causal plane choose who talks to you. They're "queuing up" to speak to you, and they know whom you need most right now.

If you happen to ask for a particular spirit guide anyway, that guide may come, or another one may show up. Trust their judgment and allow it to happen as it unfolds.

In the beginning, you might feel overwhelmed by the presence of a sacred being of high frequency in your energy field. Breathe deeply and take your time to allow your spirit guide to settle in. Embrace the opportunity with gratitude.

Depending on which of your clairsenses are most developed, you may feel the presence of a high-level spirit guide in different ways. You may hear its voice, feel your guide in your body and with your emotions, see it in a human or other form, intuitively know it is there, or even smell or taste it.

Communication with high-level spirit guides always feels loving and wonderful. If you encounter the slightest uncomfortable sensation at any time, proceed to step 10, open your eyes, and breathe deeply. Then, ground yourself again firmly, as described in Chapter 9. Please refer to Chapter 8 for more information about ensuring safety in spirit communication.

It's totally okay if you don't perceive any presence yet. Several possible causes may block your spirit communication. Thought interference and overthinking are the most common ones. Please refer to the next Chapter to learn strategies for overcoming blockages. You can do this, even if it doesn't work as expected on the first try!

Step 6

Feel free to welcome your spirit guide in your own way. Again, if you encounter any irritation or discomfort, proceed to step 10 and ground yourself.

Step 7

Congratulations, you've done a great job in the previous steps! If you feel a presence, you're now ready to talk to your high-level spirit guide, which is the essence of this book.

You may ask for your spirit guide's name and greet it. Some people get a name right away. Some get sounds and letters, which later form into a name. Others get a name only weeks after they ask for it, or never.

Don't get too fixated on getting your guide's name. It's not important to your guides. They know each other by energy patterns. If you don't get a name, you can choose a nickname for your guide or continue without naming it.

As described in Chapter 7, ask any questions that matter to you right now. Formulate the question in your mind or say it out loud.

If you don't have any specific questions, you can ask your spirit guide to tell you what matters most for you right now.

Your high-level spirit guides always send you their answers immediately. They may come in instant knowing, words, images, mind clips and movies, songs, emotions, body sensations, smells, tastes, and other ways.

Have faith and allow it to happen. Let it flow, and trust in your intuition. Your spirit guide knows exactly what is best for you.

You don't need to take notes during your spirit communication. It might distract you and interrupt your communication, weakening your connection and hindering the flow of energy and information. You'll remember everything that matters anyway.

Your spirit guide may also take you on a visual journey instead of sending single messages. Just observe, trust, and let it unfold.

Don't despair if you don't receive answers or feel you can't fully understand them. It may take some practice until you get used to this form of communication.

In that case, focus on fully experiencing your spirit guide's wonderful presence and try to ask questions again in another session.

Feel free to keep talking to your spirit guide for as long as you like. Your guide is pleased with the opportunity to speak to you and will never tire of it.

Step 8

You can express your gratitude in your own way. Your spirit guide will thank you, too, for opening up and making the effort to connect.

Step 9

While your spirit guide's energy is leaving your energy field, you might sense that a remainder of its energy will stay with you. You'll probably receive more messages and context from your spirit guide in the coming hours and days. The guidance you experience may also result in amazing synchronicities, unexpected encounters, and other positive surprises in your life.

Step 10

Give yourself enough time to return to the present moment and adjust to it.

12.
How To Overcome Blockages

Blockages may prevent you from connecting with your spirit guides or from receiving and understanding their messages. These are typical reasons for blockages in spirit communication:

Overthinking

Overthinking is the most common cause of blocked spirit communication. It refers to our brain's habit of excessively analyzing, doubting, and rationalizing the messages and sensations we receive.

Overthinkers tend to doubt their intuition, examine and scrutinize every detail, and fear making mistakes.

Overthinking hinders the free flow of information and energy between your spirit guides and decreases your focus and receptiveness.

Thought Interference

All of us are prone to the interference of thoughts in meditation and spirit communication. The more we practice, the quieter our minds become, and our ability to focus increases.

Overthinking leads to more thought interference. But even when we're not overthinking, we usually get a stream of mental chatter and random thoughts like going through our to-do list, remembering how our neighbor annoyed us earlier, worrying about our next date, planning which groceries we need to shop for, etc.

The mental noise of constant thought interference can create a barrier to connecting with your spirit guides and drown out their sometimes subtle whispers.

Emotional Disturbances

Strong negative emotions such as anxiety, anger, sadness, fear, or jealousy interfere with spirit communication. Such feelings can be present before you connect to your spirit guides or arise spontaneously during a practice session.

Strong negative emotions disrupt the energy flow in your body and aura, cloud your intuition, and lead to even more mental chatter.

Clear and receptive spirit communication is impossible when strong emotional disturbances are present.

Limiting Beliefs

Deep-seated beliefs about oneself, spirituality, or the nature of reality can be subconscious barriers to spirit communication.

Beliefs like "I'm not worthy," "I'm not sensitive," or "I'm not capable" undermine your confidence and trust in your intuitive abilities.

Such beliefs can become self-fulfilling prophecies, reinforcing thought patterns that strengthen feelings of limitation, separation, and disconnection, blocking the flow of spirit communication.

Lack of Trust

Trust is fundamental to spirit communication.

Trust in yourself and the high-level guides you communicate with is necessary to open up and receive their valuable guidance.

Fear, doubt, and skepticism create a lack of trust, blocking your spirit communication.

Ego Attachments

Our ego's attachments to identity, desires, and expectations can interfere with spirit communication by fueling cravings, aversions, or illusions of control.

Such egoic tendencies can prevent you from surrendering to the flow of the present moment and experiencing profound states of connection with your spirit guides.

Energetic Imbalances

Disruptions in your body's energy system, such as blocked chakras, stagnant energy channels, or depleted vital energy, can hinder the flow of energy required for spirit communication.

Energetic imbalances can manifest as feelings of heaviness, lethargy, scatteredness, or disconnection.

External Distractions

External stimuli such as noise or movement can disrupt spirit communication by drawing your attention away from the present moment. Such distractions can be a challenge for maintaining focus and inner stillness.

Clearly, **our minds and emotions are the source of all blockages in spirit communication**. Let's explore the best strategies for overcoming them and clearing the way toward precise conversations with your spirit guides:

1. Meditate Regularly

Meditation is the perfect companion to spirit communication and the most powerful tool for overcoming blockages.

One of the main benefits of meditation is that it trains you to cultivate inner stillness, allowing you to quiet your mind and calm your mental chatter. Your ability to focus and be still without thought interference increases the more you practice meditation and spirit communication.

Meditation enhances emotional stability by reducing anxiety, anger, fear, and other negative emotions that create barriers to spirit communication. It improves emotional well-being and promotes positive feelings such as gratitude, compassion, and joy.

Meditation enhances your self-awareness as you practice observing your thoughts, emotions, and sensations without attachment or judgment.

This heightened awareness allows you to identify and address blockages hindering your ability to connect with your spirit guides. It also allows you to become aware and let go of limiting beliefs and ego attachments.

Meditation strengthens your intuition and helps clear energetic imbalances. By practicing regularly, you become more aware of the energy flow in your body. You can cleanse, activate, and harmonize your chakras, allowing your energy to flow freely and increasing your vital energy (see chakra healing meditation in Chapter 13).

Last but not least, meditation trains you in dealing with external distractions. You learn to either blank them out or simply integrate them into your meditation without perceiving them as a hindrance anymore.

In summary, meditation helps you address and overcome the potential causes of blockages in spirit communication listed above. Committing to a daily meditation practice is highly recommended.

If you wish to do both, always meditate before your spirit communication. It'll benefit your ability to focus, receive, and interpret the messages from your guides.

Please refer to Chapter 13 for a simple daily meditation you can do for five minutes or several hours, allowing you to fit it into your schedule as required.

2. Return To The Present Moment Relentlessly

All that exists is the present moment. Future and past are only mind constructs. Everything happens now.

"Relentlessly returning to the present moment" is a 24/7 practice that has long been recommended by Advaita Vedanta teachers and recently gained popularity as "mindfulness."

This practice extends your active meditation and spirit communication sessions. It increases focus, inner stillness, stability, resilience, and happiness.

Use these three steps to practice returning to the present moment anytime and anywhere:

Step 1: Attention

Use your awareness to hold your attention without letting it get pulled away by passing thoughts.

The object of your attention doesn't matter in this respect. It can be anything from your breath, physical objects, other persons, or work projects.

What matters is that you learn to keep focusing only on one thing.

Don't be discouraged if you have to return over and over from your passing thoughts to your object of attention. That's part of the practice.

Step 2: Present Moment

While you're holding your attention, drop deeply into the present moment, into now. Just this breath. Just this moment.

Immerse yourself and soak in the present moment with everything that it offers. Stay with it, stay with one.

By dropping past and future, you also eliminate all the mental noise associated with them. You'll discover how still and peaceful your mind can become.

Step 3: No Judgement

You're the silent watcher, the awareness behind or underneath all thoughts and emotions. Nonjudgment's essence is not to go with your thoughts and create further stories in endless cycles.

If you observe the mind commenting on and labeling things while practicing, allow these thoughts to float through your awareness without clinging to or resisting them. Simply let them be.

This practice is about cultivating awareness, not about suppressing the mind or trying to stop thinking.

A peaceful state of awareness exists underneath the drone of the mind's noise. Unconditioned awareness can emerge without the mental chatter and, with it, a sense of peace, joy, and wholeness.

3. Experience Your Emotions Without Stories

The Advaita Vedanta teacher "Gangaji" offers a precious and powerful approach to self-inquiry of our negative emotions like fear, anger, or sadness.

We usually wish to experience more pleasant feelings like fun, happiness, and bliss. We tend to either repress negative feelings completely or express them somehow, hoping they'll disappear.

But neither of these strategies really works. The emotions come back when triggered, and we often create stories and judgments around them, especially stories of victimhood.

Gangaji invites us to consciously and directly meet and experience our negative emotions. To entirely drop into and to the bottom of them, letting go of all the stories and judgments we have built around them.

To find how, underneath them, an incredible treasure awaits us: peace and the true essence of our being.

Gangaji explains this approach much better in her own words. If you're attracted by it, please refer to Gangaji's blog at gangaji.org/blog for more information and search for "Gangaji emotions" on YouTube.

4. Set Your Intention

Before communicating with your spirit guides, you can set a positive intention for the session during the first few deep breaths.

This purpose can be anything from seeking clarity and guidance on a challenge to finding the answers to life's big questions.

By setting a clear and positive intention, you send a message to the spiritual planes telling them what you need and that you're open and receptive to guidance. Your intention helps to create a safe and welcoming space for your spirit guides to communicate with you.

5. Stop Overthinking

Overthinking is one of the biggest obstacles to spirit communication. Any negative thoughts can be a hindrance, whether you're worrying about your daily life or having doubts about the messages from your spirit guides.

Switching your brain off is difficult, but you can do several things to help you stop overthinking.

Firstly, when you notice that you're overanalyzing or overly doubtful, it's a perfect moment to practice returning to the present moment, as described in the last section.

Acknowledge these thoughts and watch them pass by without judgment or building stories around them.

Of course, this doesn't mean you should completely let go of your common sense and discernment during spirit communication.

Secondly, try to let go of any expectations. When you have fixed expectations about what you should be experiencing during a spirit communication session, it can be easy to get caught up in your thoughts.

Instead, release all expectations and be open to any messages coming through.

Thirdly, it's essential to trust the process. Spirit communication can be unpredictable. Trust the process and have faith that the messages you receive are really meant for you, even if you don't understand everything yet.

Fourthly, don't second-guess yourself. When you receive a message from a high-level spirit guide, don't second-guess it or try to rationalize it away.

Have faith that the transmission is genuine and try to interpret it as best you can. If you're unsure what a message means, write it down and reflect on it later.

Lastly, if you're getting frustrated or feeling stuck, take a break and return to it later. Overthinking can be exhausting, and sometimes stepping away for a little while can help you come back with a fresh perspective.

Practice surrendering to the process and releasing the need for control or validation. Trust that you're always supported, guided, and protected by your wonderful family of spirit guides, even in moments of uncertainty or doubt.

6. Clear Negative Energy

Negative energy can arise from many sources, including stress, interpersonal interactions, traumas, and repressed emotions. It can obstruct your ability to communicate with your guides.

You can clear negative energy in your meditations to over-come blockages, and with any of these methods:

- Smudge with sage, cedar, palo santo, or copal.

- Take a sea salt bath, keep a bowl of water with salt, or sprinkle your home with salt. Make sure to dispose of the salt regularly.

- Apply essential oils such as lavender, peppermint, tea tree, or sage.

- Create a crystal grid using crystals known for their puri-fying properties, such as clear quartz, rose quartz, ame-thyst, obsidian, black tourmaline, citrine, and selenite.

- Enjoy a cleansing sound healing session (see also Chapter 13).

- Declutter your living and working spaces.

- Use energy healing techniques like reiki, crystal therapy, or acupuncture.

7. Practice Gratitude

Practicing gratitude is a powerful mindset that helps us ap-preciate life more deeply and overcome blockages in spirit communication.

Embracing gratitude isn't always easy. Our brains aren't wired to make us feel happy. They're designed to help us survive, constantly looking for what's wrong as a means to protect us, often resulting in unnecessary fear and anger.

The good news is you can't feel grateful and at the same time afraid or angry. It's impossible because these are opposite patterns of focus.

Shifting your focus to gratitude can change your life! These are some ideas for practicing:

Daily Three Things in Three Minutes

Think of three things you're grateful for right now. They can be from your past, present, or future.

Picture the first one as vividly as possible, and feel the gratitude in your heart.

After about a minute, go on to the second thing, then to the third. These things can be big or simple, like a child's smile or someone saying "thank you" to you.

Even on your worst days, you can find something small and meaningful to be grateful for. It's a good idea to make this three-minute practice a part of your morning routine.

Express Gratitude to Others

Make it a habit to express gratitude. Say thank you to people who help you, or send them a note via text or email.

Give them a big hug if appropriate. Give compliments. Listen attentively and show empathy. Show appreciation for your loved ones by acknowledging their contributions, qualities, and support. Pay it forward by performing acts of kindness. Smile!

Write a Gratitude Journal

Write down things you are grateful for. Reflect on the positive aspects of your life, such as relationships, experiences, accomplishments, and simple pleasures. Writing them down helps to reinforce feelings of appreciation and abundance.

Use Visual Reminders

Place reminders of gratitude in your environment, such as inspirational quotes, photos of loved ones, or objects with special meaning. Use these reminders to pause and reflect on what you're thankful for.

Volunteer or Give Back

Engage in acts of service or kindness to others to express gratitude for the blessings in your life. Volunteering, donating to charity, or helping someone in need fosters a sense of connection.

Practice Gratitude in Challenging Times

Even during difficult moments, look for silver linings or lessons to be grateful for. Remind yourself of the positive aspects of your life and the resources you have to overcome obstacles.

Shift your perspective from what's lacking to what's present and valuable in your life.

Celebrate Progress

Acknowledge and celebrate your personal growth, achievements, and milestones. Recognize the effort and perseverance that went into reaching them, and express gratitude for the journey.

8. Use Incantations

Incantations are a powerful technique promoted by the American author, coach and speaker Tony Robbins.

Most people know about affirmations, words of encouragement you speak to yourself. The problem with affirmations is that they often fail.

While they sound positive, they won't carry the transformative power if you don't honestly believe in the thoughts and meaning behind them. I tried affirmations intensely in some of my darkest times and failed miserably because they simply didn't ring true.

With incantations, you are not only speaking words of empowerment but also using your body and voice. You change your physiology and state, leading to a different, positive outlook.

If you repeat incantations regularly, your body and mind store them permanently as they reverberate throughout. You can use Tony's kind of incantations and create your own.

Search for "Tony Robbins incantations" on YouTube for more information.

9. Strengthen Your Intuition

Intuition is a crucial component of spirit communication, as it helps you sense and interpret the messages from your guides. Practicing meditation and spirit communication will strengthen your intuition.

There are many further ways of training and developing your intuition, such as:

Trust Your Gut Feelings

Be aware of your gut feelings or "hunches" and learn to trust them, even if they initially don't seem rational or logical. If you're like me, you can probably list countless times when you regretted not listening to your guts.

Connect With Nature.

Spend time in nature to quieten your mind, reconnect with your inner self, and attune to the Earth's natural rhythms.

Nature has a way of grounding and centering us, making it easier to access our intuition.

Journaling

Keep a journal to record messages from your spirit guides as well as intuitive insights, dreams, synchronicities, and experiences.

Read your past journal entries occasionally and reflect on them to deepen your understanding of your intuition.

Practice Intuitive Drawing And Writing

Doodle or draw without any specific plan or intention. Let your intuition guide your hand and see what images or symbols emerge on the paper.

Or connect with your guidance and write down whatever comes to mind without censoring or analyzing it.

Look at your drawings and writings a few days later and reflect on them.

Trust Your Body

Pay attention to physical sensations and signals from your body, such as tingles, chills, or knots in your stomach.

Your body often communicates intuitive information that can guide you in decision-making.

Practice Patience and Persistence

Strengthening your intuition and communicating with your spirit guides is a lifelong journey that requires practice, patience, and persistence.

Be patient with yourself and the process. Trust that your intuitive abilities will continue to improve over time.

Don't expect to receive only precise messages from your guides or to immediately have profound spiritual experiences. Focus on building your relationship with your intuition and spirit guides over time.

10. Seek Support

Don't hesitate to seek support if you struggle to overcome blockages. Mental and emotional health are complex and multifaceted.

Seeking support from mental health professionals, counselors, mentors, or spiritual advisors can be essential for your healing and growth.

Feel free to join our community (see last page) and other spiritual groups to meet like-minded people.

13.
Going Deeper Toward Constant Connection

You'll embark on an **accelerated spiritual growth path** by working with your high-level spirit guides and following their advice.

They'll help you create experiences of more joy, confidence, and awareness of who you are in the present moment. They'll assist you in your spiritual awakening.

You'll notice gradual changes and shifts in your life with regular practice. They may not be drastic, but you'll get to know yourself in new ways over time.

Please don't expect your spirit guides to solve all your problems for you. They allow you to see more clearly and accept your challenges as growth opportunities.

They'll gladly advise you, but you still need to learn your lessons and make your own decisions of free will.

As you practice talking to your spirit guides actively using the "Ten-Step Method" more often, you'll also become conscious of receiving their messages outside your active sessions.

Over time, this can result in a **constant connection and communication** with your high-level spirit guides, whereby you receive instant replies to any question you ponder.

Constant connection is a wonderful state that allows exceptional experiences and encounters to happen in your daily life. The main requirement is to always remain open and at high frequency.

A constant relationship with your spirit guides also increases your empathy toward others. Your heart and soul open up to the human messengers and mirrors around you.

Amazing synchronicities may happen at any moment in your life when you keep the communication channel open and follow the advice given to you.

Simultaneously, you learn to set healthy boundaries and ensure no one tramples over them.

The more you increase your frequency, the easier it becomes to go deeper toward constant connection. Many factors influence your vibration and frequency.

Firstly, please review the strategies listed in Chapter 12 for overcoming blockages in spirit communication.

They also help you to increase your frequency permanently, especially meditating, returning to the present moment relentlessly, and experiencing your emotions without judgment and stories.

This chapter provides you with additional information and ideas you can focus on to increase your frequency and walk on your sacred spiritual path.

1. Meditation

Regular meditation helps increase your frequency and reduce mental chatter. Stay focused in your meditation sessions, strengthen your connection with your spiritual guidance, and stay grounded in a world of distractions.

If you don't follow a regular meditation practice yet, you can use this basic and simple but very effective meditation that an extraordinary Advaita Vedanta teacher taught me:

Step 1:

Sit comfortably in a quiet space where you won't be disturbed, ideally in your "sacred space." You can sit on a meditation cushion or a chair. Don't lie down.

Step 2:

Close your eyes and take several slow, deep breaths. Inhale profoundly into your stomach, filling it with air from the bottom like a vase fills with water.

When exhaling, let go of the air effortlessly and reversely, from top to bottom. Feel the breath entering and leaving your body, allowing yourself to relax with each exhale.

Keep focusing your attention on how you slowly breathe in and out. If thoughts interfere, let them go again and return to the present moment.

Step 3:

Fold your hands in front of your stomach. Let them rest comfortably in your lap.

Direct your attention to the warmth between your folded hands. Stay there with your awareness and attention.

Thoughts will arise, maybe emotions too. Whenever you realize you are getting caught up in a thought, gently bring your awareness back to the warmth between your hands.

Be with one. Rest your attention in the space between your thoughts in the warmth between your hands.

Observe and allow things to be as they are without needing to fix or change anything.

Fold your hands like this pose, but let them rest comfortably in your lap to hold the position without muscular effort.

You can stay in this space for as long as you like.

It can be wonderful to take guided meditation journeys, but this simple basic meditation is all that's needed. It's more effective than guided meditations for reducing mental chatter as well as increasing your vibration and receptiveness.

Step 4:

When you feel ready, gently return to the present moment. Wiggle your fingers and toes, stretch your body, and open your eyes. Express gratitude.

2. Chakra Healing

Our chakras are the centers of our bodies' energy system along the spine.

"Chakra' literally means "wheel" in Sanskrit. Each chakra is a rotating energy vortex that radiates energy in an outward spiral into the related organs of the body and further.

All chakras are in an optimum state when they're healthy and active, spinning clockwise at a medium speed and in balance with each other.

Chakras move clockwise to push energy out of our body and counterclockwise to pull energy in from the external world and people in it.

The frequency of our chakric vibrations determines the strength and direction of our energy flow. The condition of your chakras influences your daily life to be in or out of balance.

Healing and balancing your chakras is crucial for your physical, mental, and spiritual health and growth. You can practice the following chakra meditation anytime to activate and align your chakras. It uses sacred "Bija mantras" or "seed mantras" from the Sanskrit language.

Step 1:

Sit comfortably in a quiet space where you won't be disturbed, ideally in your "sacred space." You can sit on a meditation cushion or a chair. Don't lie down.

Step 2:

Close your eyes and take several slow, deep breaths. Inhale profoundly into your stomach, filling it with air from the bottom like a vase fills with water.

When exhaling, let go of the air effortlessly and reversely, from top to bottom. Feel the breath entering and leaving your body, allowing yourself to relax with each exhale.

Make sure you're well-grounded. If needed, do the grounding meditation from Chapter 9 first. If thoughts interfere, let them go again and return to the present moment.

Step 3:

Direct your attention to the **root** chakra at the base of your spine. Exhale into it while visualizing **red** power energy at that location in your body in the form of an energy ball or vortex.

Start chanting the mantra "**LAM**" with every exhale while imagining how the red energy in your root chakra that you breathe into grows brighter and stronger, filling you with vitality and strength.

When you feel that your root chakra is fully activated, slowly start reducing it again to the size of your fist. Feel how it's spinning in your body in a clockwise direction. Direct it patiently to do so if needed.

Step 4:

Direct your attention to the **sacral** chakra below your navel, in the middle of your spine. Exhale into it while visualizing **orange** energy at that location in your body in the form of an energy ball or vortex.

Start chanting the mantra **"VAM"** with every exhale while imagining how the energy in your sacral chakra grows brighter and stronger, filling you with creativity and sensuality.

Perhaps you can feel an orange sun lighting up your stomach, intestines, and other organs from inside. When your orange sacral chakra is fully activated, slowly start reducing it again to the size of your fist.

Feel it spinning in your body clockwise, in sync with the root chakra. Direct it patiently to do so if needed. Stay with the sensation of both activated chakras for a few breaths.

Step 5:

Direct your attention to the **solar plexus** chakra behind your physical solar plexus in the middle of your spine. Exhale into it while visualizing **yellow** energy at that location in your body in the form of an energy ball or vortex.

Start chanting the mantra **"RAM"** with every exhale while imagining how the yellow energy in your upper abdomen grows brighter and stronger, giving you the confidence and courage to pursue your goals.

The solar plexus chakra is a yellow sun of inner strength. When you feel it's fully activated, slowly start reducing it again to the size of your fist.

Feel it spinning in your body clockwise, in sync with the lower two chakras. Stay with the sensation of all three activated chakras spinning in sync for a few breaths.

Step 6:

Direct your attention to the **heart** chakra in the middle of your chest, near your physical heart. Exhale into it while visualizing **green** energy at that location in your body in the form of an energy ball or vortex.

Start chanting the mantra **"YAM"** with every exhale while imagining how the green energy in your chest grows brighter and stronger, filling your heart with love and compassion for yourself and others.

Feel how the green power of your heart chakra opens your heart. When it's fully activated, slowly start reducing it again to the size of your fist.

Feel it spinning in your body clockwise, in sync with the lower three chakras. Stay with the sensation of all four activated chakras spinning in sync for a few breaths.

Step 7:

Direct your attention to the **throat** chakra in the middle of your throat. Exhale into it while visualizing **light blue** energy at that location in your body in the form of an energy ball or vortex.

Start chanting the mantra **"HAM"** with every exhale while imagining how the light blue energy in your upper abdomen grows brighter and stronger, allowing you to speak your truth with clarity and confidence.

The throat chakra is a light blue sun of expression. When it's fully activated, slowly start reducing it again to the size of your fist.

Feel it spinning in your body clockwise, in sync with the lower four chakras. Stay with the sensation of all five activated chakras spinning in sync for a few breaths.

Step 8:

Direct your attention to the **third eye** chakra in the middle of your head at the height of the third eye between your eyebrows. Exhale into it while visualizing **dark blue** energy at that location in your body in the form of an energy ball or vortex.

Start chanting the mantra **"OM"** with every exhale while imagining how the dark blue energy in your upper abdomen grows brighter and stronger, allowing you to see clearly and access your spiritual guidance.

The third eye chakra is a dark blue sun of imagination. When it's fully activated, slowly start reducing it again to the size of your fist.

Feel it spinning in your body clockwise, in sync with the lower five chakras. Stay with the sensation of all six activated chakras spinning in sync for a few breaths.

Step 9:

Direct your attention to the **crown** chakra on top of your head. Exhale into it while visualizing **violet or white** energy at that location in your body in the form of an energy ball or vortex.

Start chanting the mantra **"AH"** with every exhale while imagining how the violet energy on top of your head grows brighter and stronger, connecting you to the entire Universe.

The crown chakra is a violet sun of consciousness. Feel it growing from the top of your head into the sky. When it's fully activated, slowly start reducing it again to the size of your fist.

Feel it spinning in your body clockwise, in sync with the lower six chakras.

Stay with the sensation of all seven activated chakras spinning in sync for as long as you like.

Step 10:

When you feel ready, gently return to the present moment. Wiggle your fingers and toes, stretch your body, and open your eyes. Express gratitude.

The spinal series Kundalini Yoga routine at the end of the next section also helps activate your chakras.

3. Yoga and Other Exercises

Yoga, meditation, and spirit communication are a perfect trilogy of activities that benefit each other. Practicing Yoga offers various advantages through its holistic approach to integrating mind, body, and soul.

Yoga helps balance our chakras and facilitates a smoother energy flow throughout the body. It also supports purifying the body and mind, releasing tension, stress, and emotional blockages.

Yoga strengthens your body and results in higher energy and brighter moods. It increases mindfulness, allowing your mind to become more still.

There are many excellent yoga teachers almost everywhere. If you haven't practiced yoga yet, try some studios in your area and find out which style suits you best.

You'll find various excellent Yoga routines on YouTube and other sites if you prefer to practice at home. I practice at least one 30-minute routine daily. Search for "Kundalini yoga spinal series" and "Ashtanga short form" to find my two favorite routines.

If Yoga is not your thing, other sports and physical activities also help you stay more grounded, joyful, and connected to the spirit world.

4. Nutrition

There's a lot of truth to the phrase, "You are what you eat." Healthy and fresh nutrition increases your vibration and your well-being.

It's up to you to determine which diet is best for you. Reducing sugar intake and eating more fresh, light, and wholesome food will support your efforts with any diet.

There are many good resources on healthy nutrition. If you don't know where to start, you can take a free online test to determine your predominant Ayurvedic Dosha type. Then, research the recommended nutrition for your type and apply it.

Another critical factor is eating less. In the Western world, we're used to overeating, and we typically have our meals at set times instead of when we're hungry. Try to eat only when you're hungry and choose smaller portions.

5. Fasting

Fasting takes the concept of eating less a step further. It's highly beneficial for your health and can help raise your frequency.

If you have no experience yet, you can experiment with intermittent fasting first. The 16/8 method of intermittent fasting involves fasting for 16 hours each day and restricting your eating window to 8 hours.

For example, you might eat between 12:00 p.m. and 8:00 p.m. and fast from 8:00 p.m. to 12:00 p.m. the next day. Some people extend this to 18/6, restricting their eating window to 6 hours.

Another intermittent fasting method is OMAD, which stands for "one meal a day." It involves eating most or all of your daily calories in a single meal.

You can combine OMAD with 16/8 or 18/6 by eating one main meal and later a snack toward the end of your eating window. Or you can try pure OMAD, which is 23/1.

Stay hydrated during fasting periods by drinking plenty of water, herbal tea, or other non-caloric beverages. Proper hydration helps curb hunger and supports your body's functions.

Consistency is required for seeing results with intermittent fasting. Try to stick to your fasting and eating schedule as consistently as possible, but also be flexible and willing to adjust based on your needs and circumstances.

If you like intermittent fasting and get good results, consider going for longer fasts occasionally.

One option is juice fasting, which involves consuming only fresh fruit and vegetable juices for a certain period. Juice fasting provides essential nutrients while giving your digestive system a break.

The most beneficial method is water fasting. It involves drinking only water for several days, usually supplemented by an intake of electrolytes without sugar.

It sounds hard, but most people find it much easier than they thought once they tried it. Besides increasing your frequency, water fasting has various other benefits, such as

- **Autophagy**: The process by which cells remove damaged or dysfunctional components and recycle them for energy. Autophagy kicks in after 2-3 days of water fasting and helps protect against many diseases.

- **Reduced Inflammation**: Chronic inflammation is linked to numerous health problems. Water fasting reduces inflammation markers in the body, lowering the risk of inflammatory diseases and supporting the respective healing processes.

- **Cellular Repair**: During fasting, the body enters a state of ketosis, burning fat for fuel instead of glucose. This metabolic shift triggers cellular repair processes, including DNA repair and the production of antioxidant enzymes.

- **Heart Health**: Water fasting improves cardiovascular health by lowering blood pressure, triglycerides, LDL cholesterol, and other risk factors for heart disease. It can also promote the growth of new blood vessels and improve circulation.

- **Immune Function**: Fasting boosts immune function by regenerating immune cells and reducing inflammation. It also increases the production of stem cells, which play a vital role in immune system maintenance.

- **Digestive Health**: Giving the digestive system a break during fasting allows it to rest and repair, which improves gut health and alleviates digestive issues like bloating, gas, and constipation.

- **Detoxification**: Water fasting supports the body's natural detoxification processes by allowing the liver and kidneys to eliminate toxins and metabolic waste products more efficiently.

- **Brain Health**: Fasting supports brain health and cognitive function by stimulating the production of brain-derived neurotrophic factor, a protein that promotes the growth and repair of neurons. It may also protect against neurodegenerative diseases like Alzheimer's and Parkinson's.

- **Mental Clarity**: Water fasting increases mental clarity and focus, especially after the first three days. This effect is due to the metabolic switch to ketosis and the release of endorphins and other neurochemicals that promote well-being.

- **Spiritual Benefits**: Almost all religions and spiritual practices promote fasting for spiritual purposes. Besides mental clarity, it can provide a sense of inner peace and connection to yourself, especially when combined with yoga, meditation, and spirit communication.

I was scared before my first water fast and thought I'd never make it. However, I was determined to try it and discovered it was much easier than I had assumed.

I now water fast for 1-2 weeks at least once a year. I consider it regular maintenance for my body. From day four onwards, I become extremely clear and receptive in my meditation and spirit communication. This effect often lasts much longer than the water fast.

6. Quick Reconnections

You can reconnect with your spirit guides anywhere and anytime. It only takes a couple of minutes. You can do this to get a specific reply you need or simply to recharge your spiritual batteries.

Use these five simple steps for quick reconnections and extend them as you like if you have more time:

1. Close your eyes and take at least three deep and slow breaths.

2. Ground yourself and feel the connection to Mother Earth.

3. Visualize your entire family of spirit guides and open up to their presence. Feel their love. Be receptive to any immediate messages they might send you.

4. Express gratitude toward your spirit guides, thanking them for their love, blessings, guidance, and support.

5. Take a few more deep breaths. Then open your eyes and return to the present moment, knowing that your guides always remain connected to you.

Quick reconnections strengthen the relationship with your spirit guides. They're comparable to quick phone calls or text messages with your partner, expressing your love between your get-togethers.

You can make a quick reconnection a part of your morning and evening routine, alternatively to your more extended sessions, and you can also reconnect quickly anytime during the day.

7. Morning Ritual

A morning ritual is essential for putting you in a grateful, positive, and empowered state that carries through your day.

Your personal morning ritual can become a powerful tool for increasing your frequency, reducing stress, achieving mental clarity, and relaxing. Committing to a consistent morning routine creates a solid foundation for your spiritual and personal growth.

It's up to you to experiment and define what works best for you. A morning ritual can last from 5 minutes to several hours, depending on how early you get up and how much time you have available before your daily chores.

Besides yoga, meditation, and spirit communication, some ideas for your morning ritual are working out, journaling, reading books, listening to podcasts or music, practicing incantations, drawing, singing, connecting with nature, taking a cold shower, practicing gratitude, setting daily goals, and contemplating your personal and spiritual development.

To give you an idea, my morning ritual consists of seven steps. Of course, you don't have to copy it exactly. Your preferences may be very different.

1. Yoga session (30 minutes)

2. Meditation practice (30-45 minutes)

3. Reconnection with my spirit guides (about 10-15 minutes; as described in the last section, I set my intention and ask them for support for my activities on this day)

4. Gratefulness (about 5 minutes; three things in three minutes, and expression of gratitude toward the people around me)

5. Incantations (5-10 minutes)

6. Dancing (5-10 minutes)

7. Cold shower (5 minutes)

It takes me at least 1,5 hours, but it's worth every minute of my time as it has tremendously improved my health and quality of life.

I don't check my phone, email, and social media before finishing this morning ritual to keep my brain undistracted.

I adjust it to the time I have available. Sometimes, I need to shorten it. At other times, I go for an extended spirit communication session. If not, I usually do my main spirit communication session around 6 p.m.

8. Evening Ritual

Following an evening ritual helps you relax your mind and body and prepare for restful sleep. Aim to go to bed and wake up at the same time each day to regulate your body's internal clock.

About an hour before bedtime, begin winding down by unplugging from electronic devices such as smartphones, computers, and TVs.

The blue light emitted by screens can disrupt your body's natural sleep cycle. Avoiding them before bedtime is highly recommended.

Like the morning ritual, it's up to you to determine what works best for you before going to sleep.

Popular evening ritual elements are similar to those of the morning ritual: meditation, spirit communication, yoga, practicing gratitude, journaling, reading, hot bubble baths or showers, etc.

The main goal of your evening ritual is to establish a consistent pattern of getting enough sleep, which is extremely important for our health and helps you increase your frequency.

9. Dance

Music is magic, and dancing to your favorite tunes is more than a fun way to move. It offers numerous benefits for your physical, mental, emotional, and spiritual health.

Dancing not only gets you in tune with your body, it also boosts your mental health. It helps reduce stress, anxiety, and depression. It can increase your self-confidence and self-esteem.

Dancing grounds you in the here and now. It can also strengthen your connection to the spiritual planes.

So, dance like nobody is watching at home alone, in the open air, or at a club with friends!

10. Nature

Wherever you live, spending time in nature increases your spiritual health and helps increase your vibration.

Even just a few minutes of watching the birds, the trees swaying in the wind, or the waves crashing on the shoreline help you to be present here and now at a higher vibration.

11. Sound Healing

Sound healing uses vibrations, frequencies, and rhythms to heal and relax your body, mind, and spirit. Exposure to harmonious sounds can restore balance and harmony to your energy systems.

Various techniques and instruments are used in sound healing, like singing bowls, tuning forks, gongs, drums, and vocal toning.

Sound healing induces deep relaxation, helping to reduce stress, anxiety, and tension. It can alleviate physical pain and discomfort by releasing endorphins, the body's natural painkillers.

It also improves sleep quality by inducing deep relaxation and releasing melatonin, the hormone responsible for regulating sleep-wake cycles.

The vibrations and frequencies of sound penetrate deep into your subconscious mind, helping you process and release stored emotions and trauma. Sound healing enhances mental clarity, focus, and concentration by calming the mind and reducing mental chatter.

Sound healing combined with meditation and visualization also helps to activate and align your chakras, clear blockages, and restore optimal energy flow.

Experiment with creating healing sounds yourself, or use YouTube or visit a professional.

12. Reduce Screen Time

Smartphones, tablets, computers, and TV screens are omnipresent nowadays. Reducing unnecessary screen time helps your mind become calmer and more present in the moment, supporting your spiritual growth.

You don't need to quit social media or your Netflix subscription altogether. Just become more aware of how much time you spend glued to screens and how it keeps your mind busy.

Don't scroll social media aimlessly or watch TV or Netflix only out of boredom. Instead, find educational, spiritual, and positive resources online and get off your screens more often.

13. Reduce News Consumption

Most news outlets overwhelm us with hourly cycles of bad news and fresh waves of outrage.

Your subconscious mind can't distinguish between what's happening in real life and what you watch and read online and offline.

Reducing your news consumption can greatly benefit your spiritual growth. It's not about blanking out what happens in the world. You can still follow that on the surface if you wish.

It's about becoming aware of your time consuming news and how it affects you. Choose wisely where you want to invest your attention.

14. Practice Spirit Communication Frequently

Frequent practice not only leads to your spirit communication becoming deeper and clearer.

Regular contact with high-frequency spiritual beings raises your vibration permanently, allowing you to implement positive changes in your life and grow spiritually.

Ask your spirit guides about what's essential for YOU to increase your frequency!

14.
Frequently Asked Questions (FAQ)

Are the messages you receive just your imagination?

This is the biggest question our doubtful minds ask when communicating with spirit guides.

High-level spirit guides are in a vibration of pure love. You'll feel it in your heart if the messages you receive genuinely come from a high-level spirit guide.

If you told your imagination to say the message, you'd feel it in your head.

Jesus said, "By their fruits, you shall know them." If you receive any guidance that is loving and wise, the results will be excellent when you follow their advice. If the results harm you, the guidance could have come from your imagination or ego.

Listen to your heart. It knows the truth. Trust your heart and intuition to discern if the messages you receive genuinely come from your loving spirit guides.

Do spirit guides truly exist?

Yes. While their existence can't be scientifically proven, thousands of matching personal accounts prove it.

You'll know they exist once you connect more often with your high-level spirit guides and talk to them.

Can you ask your spirit guides anything?

Yes, you can ask your spirit guides literally anything. They'll immediately give you their best answer, even to simple, mundane questions.

If you ask them something they can't reply to, like a future prediction, they'll tell you so. Their goal is to assist you in the best way possible for your soul's evolution.

Do spirit guides know your future?

No. The future is not predetermined.

Your future is co-created through thoughts and actions of your own free will and that of others. High-level spirit guides respect your free will and don't predict the future. They work alongside you in this co-creation process.

They understand potential paths and outcomes based on your current energy and trajectory. They can show you likely future scenarios and consequences of your decisions of today.

What do our spirit guides know about us?

Everything. High-level spirit guides have complete and immediate access to the Akashic records, also called the "Universal Library."

All universal events, thoughts, words, emotions, and actions of all entities and life forms from the past, present, and potential future are stored in the Akashic records.

Thus, your high-level guides know everything you have ever thought, felt, said, done, or dreamt. But they'll never judge you, so there is no reason for you to be ashamed of anything from your past.

Can you see your spirit guides?

Some of us see their spirit guides through their sense of clair-voyance. You might see a general vision, a clear picture, or even a mental movie showing your guide.

High-level spirit guides can show themselves in different forms or not at all. Those who are ascended masters may use a form from one of their earthly lives.

Don't despair if you can't see your guides with your inner eyes. Your clairsenses may instead let you hear, feel, smell, taste their presence, or instinctively know about it.

Are your spirit guides ignoring you?

Your high-level spirit guides never ignore you. They're always there for you and have supported you since your birth.

Receiving their messages and guidance only depends on your state.

I have worked with several persons who believed in being ig-nored by their spirit guides. Once they learned to apply the "Ten-Step Method," they connected successfully with their guides and got rid of that belief.

Does everyone have spirit guides?

Yes. Every human being has several high-level spirit guides and angels actively supporting them.

Can you have more than one spirit guide?

Yes, you have a whole family of high-level spirit guides. Some are with you for your lifetime, others only for specific periods or challenges.

What's the difference between higher self and spirit guides?

The higher self is a part of your soul. It represents your highest potential, purpose, and truth. It's connected to the divine source.

Your earthly personality is just a tiny part of the total self. You're always united with your higher self through your subconscious, intuition, dreams, visions, and psychic senses.

Your spirit guides are different souls at different frequencies. They're not part of your higher self.

However, they work together with your higher self to allow you to experience love and freedom, learn the spiritual lessons your soul chose for this incarnation, and walk on your path toward Self-Realization.

Can my spirit guides interact with my friend's spirit guide?

Yes, high-level spirit guides interact with each other. As they aren't constrained by time and space, they communicate instantly to support the highest good for all involved.

Your spirit guides may collaborate with the spirit guides of your relatives and friends. This interaction can occur for various reasons, such as facilitating soul connections, supporting mutual growth, or assisting in shared endeavors and challenges.

Can you talk to your spirit guides whenever you want?

Absolutely. Your high-level spirit guides always support you, send you messages, and induce synchronicities for you.

Tune in to listen by initiating active communication sessions using the "Ten-Step Method."

I only get whispers from my guides that I don't understand

Don't despair. It's great if you already perceive their presence.

Continue practicing and apply the strategies listed in Chapters 12 and 13 to overcome blockages and increase your frequency.

Are there 8 billion spirit guides?

We don't know how many spirit guides exist. This question stems from the belief that every human has one exclusive spirit guide only for himself.

That belief is countered by the ability of highly evolved spirit guides to communicate with unlimited human souls simultaneously, as well as our ability to connect with several spirit guides. There is no exclusivity in relationships with spirit guides.

Is spirit communication dangerous?

Spirit communication can only be dangerous if you connect with low-frequency spiritual entities from the astral plane. They may seek to deceive, manipulate, or cause harm if you don't communicate with the right intention, protection, and discernment.

If you apply the "Ten-Step Method" correctly, you'll never connect with such less-evolved entities.

Please consult Chapter 8 on how to deal with such entities.

Always maintain a healthy sense of skepticism and critical thinking to discern between genuine high-level spiritual guidance and possible deceptive influences.

Do spirit guides lie sometimes?

High-level spirit guides from the causal plane will never lie to you.

Only very low-frequency spiritual entities from the astral plane may try to deceive you and lie; see the last reply.

Can spirit guides possess you?

High-level spirit guides would never try to possess you in any way, and even the lowest-level spirit entities would only be able to possess you if you permit them to do so.

15.
Community & Contact Details

Thank you for reading my book all the way to the last page! It would mean the world to me if you **post a quick and honest review on Amazon or Goodreads**.

As a bonus for purchasing this book, you're invited to join my private spirit communication community. It's a safe and welcoming space to ask questions, share experiences, and connect with like-minded practitioners. Please use this link to request your exclusive access:

talktoyourspiritguides.com/community

Let's talk if you need help implementing the content of this book. Use any of these options to contact me:

- Book a free discovery call:

  talktoyourspiritguides.com/call

- Book a one-on-one online spirit communication training:

  talktoyourspiritguides.com/training

- Send me an email: will@talktoyourspiritguides.com

- Text me on WhatsApp:

  talktoyourspiritguides.com/whatsapp

I wish you lots of joy and spiritual growth on your spirit communication journey.

With love and reverence,
Will